SYMPTOMATIC

TO

SYSTEMIC

SYMPTOMATIC

TO

SYSTEMIC

UNDERSTANDING POSTWAR CYCLES
AND FINANCIAL DEBACLES

GREENLEAF
BOOK GROUP PRESS

This publication is designed to provide accurate and authoritative information in regard to the subject matter covered. It is sold with the understanding that the publisher and author are not engaged in rendering professional services. If expert assistance is required, the services of a competent professional should be sought.

Published by Greenleaf Book Group Press
Austin, Texas
www.gbgpress.com

Distributed by Greenleaf Book Group

For ordering information or special discounts for bulk purchases, please contact Greenleaf Book Group at PO Box 91869, Austin, TX 78709, 512.891.6100.

Design and composition by Greenleaf Book Group
Cover design by Greenleaf Book Group and Sheila Parr
Cover image ©iStockphoto / yamonstro
The table on page 164 is reprinted with permission from JPMorgan Chase & Co.
© 1978 All rights reserved.

Publisher's Cataloging-in-Publication data is available.

Print ISBN: 978-1-62634-594-2

eBook ISBN: 978-1-62634-595-9

Part of the Tree Neutral® program, which offsets the number of trees consumed in the production and printing of this book by taking proactive steps, such as planting trees in direct proportion to the number of trees used: www.treeneutral.com

Printed in the United States of America on acid-free paper

18 19 20 21 22 23 24   10 9 8 7 6 5 4 3 2 1

First Edition

Contents

PREFACE vii

INTRODUCTION 1

SECTION 1   What Is a Business Cycle? 7

CHAPTER 1   The 1948–1949 First Postwar Recession 13

CHAPTER 2   The 1953–1954 Post-Korean War Recession 23

CHAPTER 3   The 1957–1958 Eisenhower Recession 35

CHAPTER 4   The 1960–1961 Rolling Adjustment Recession 43

CHAPTER 5   The 1969–1970 Nixon Recession 53

CHAPTER 6   The 1973–1975 Oil Crisis Recession 65

CHAPTER 7   The January to July 1980
Carter Credit Control Recession 77

CHAPTER 8   The 1981–1982 Iranian Energy Crisis Recession 87

CHAPTER 9   The July 1990–March 1991 Gulf War Recession 97

CHAPTER 10   The March 2001–November 2001 9/11 Recession 107

CHAPTER 11   The December 2007–June 2009 Subprime Recession 119

SUMMARY Postwar Business Cycles in Brief 131

SECTION 2 Evolution of Financial Debacles 135

CHAPTER 12 Financial Dislocations and the Business Cycle 143

CHAPTER 13 From Small to Large to Systemically Important 161

CHAPTER 14 From One-Off to Industry and Sector-Wide Dislocations .. 179

CHAPTER 15 Corporate Governance Credit Cycle 191

CHAPTER 16 Subprime Credit Cycle 201

CHAPTER 17 International Financial Crises and
Their Link to US Debacles 221

CONCLUSION 237

ACKNOWLEDGMENTS 245

ABOUT THE AUTHOR 247

Preface

Interpretations of what caused the Great Depression range from the traditional Keynesian view of a collapse in aggregate demand, to the monetarist focus on the 35 percent contraction in money. More recently, the role of debt deflation has been identified as the cause of the Great Depression. The concept is basically that loose credit standards led to overindebtedness, fueling speculation and asset bubbles that caused a collapse in credit and the banking system when the bubble burst. Throughout the entirety of the Great Depression, an estimated more than nine thousand US banks failed—by far the worst stretch in domestic history, regarding bank failures. The debt deflation interpretation of the Great Depression coincides with the meltdown experienced between 2007 and 2009. A bubble in home prices resulted in an explosion in debt that fueled the bubble, and when defaults picked up, the collapse brought down the banking industry and damaged the household sector's balance sheet.

These two banking crises frame our analysis of postwar business cycles and the evolution of financial dislocations associated with them. Analyzing each cycle and how banks fared through the downturn leads to an important conclusion.

Specifically, the nature of the credit cycle associated with recessions changed during the 1990–1991 recession from those experienced over the prior forty years. The latest three business cycles, in fact, have been led or amplified by the forced restructuring of a key macro balance sheet. These include the collapse of the thrift industry, the restructuring of the nonfinancial corporate balance sheet, and more recently, the collapse of the banking industry and the deterioration in the household balance sheet.

The financial dislocations between these two systemic collapses (1929–1933 and 2007–2009) range from simple one-off local bank failures caused by check fraud or embezzlement, to the collapse of a major regional bank in the wake of fraud and declining energy prices, to the near collapse of a money center bank on the back of bad emerging market loans. Besides these domestic bank problems, the 1997 Asian financial crisis and the 1998 Russian default precipitated the failure of a major hedge fund that eventually required recapitalization from sixteen major global financial institutions orchestrated by Federal Reserve Chairman Alan Greenspan and Treasury Secretary Robert Rubin. As such, important lessons can be learned by identifying the bank failures associated with each downturn in the economy in order to understand the important role banks played in each of the postwar business cycles, and to understand how financial dislocations have evolved from the resulting contraction in the economy which caused the recession.

Introduction

The 2007–2009 recession was abnormally long and deep. It lasted eighteen months, the longest of the postwar period. Real gross domestic product (GDP) tumbled by 4.2 percent, from peak to trough, while the civilian jobless rate climbed from a low of 4.4 percent during the 2001–2007 expansion to a cyclical high of 10 percent.

Besides being long and deep, the 2007–2009 recession was followed by a halting recovery that lasted several years. It required new and innovative policy initiatives by the Federal Reserve and Congress before the corner was turned and the expansion took hold. But the most noteworthy aspect of the "Great Recession" was its cause. Most business cycles of the postwar period resulted from the Fed tightening rates to rein in inflation, whereas deteriorating credit conditions are universally accepted as the cause of the 2007–2009 downturn in the economy. The subprime crisis, in fact, was triggered by a rating agency downgrade of a select group of derivative securities that precipitated a sharp deterioration in the household sector's balance sheet. This balance sheet deterioration then spread to the domestic banking industry, and eventually spread overseas—Contagion—and resulted in a truly global financial crisis and recession.

The evolution from inflation-driven business cycles to credit-induced cycles reflects the transition from credit debacles being symptomatic of a recession, to becoming systemic in nature. This evolution reflects the movement of the economy from being driven by excess demand, to being dominated by excess supply. The structural changes in the economy and the regulatory framework imposed on the economy, as well as the changes in the financial markets that have unfolded during the postwar period, have also driven this shift from inflation to credit cycles.

Tracing the evolution of financial crises/debacles through the postwar period strongly suggests that credit cycles are here to stay—especially if excess supply conditions dominate both the product and labor markets. The Federal Reserve and the Bank for International Settlements seem to understand this shift in the nature of business cycles, even though there has been little discussion of this intrinsic shift in the economy by market participants or in the financial press. The "counter-cyclical capital buffer" is an example of new regulation designed to help address the reality of changing credit conditions leading business cycles, instead of being led by inflationary imbalances on the product side of the economy.

Inflation cycles typically occur as an economic recovery matures into an expansion. Capacity constraints begin to be stretched in both the product and labor markets, leading to accelerating inflation. Demand exceeds supply, and the prices of goods and services begin to rise. Accelerating inflation erodes purchasing power, and leads to a declining dollar, further reinforcing the acceleration in prices. The Federal Reserve is eventually forced to break this cycle by hiking short-term rates and rationing liquidity in the economy.

A credit recession is fundamentally different from an inflation cycle. In a world dominated by excess supply, inflation fails to heat up as the business cycle matures, so interest rates stay low, and eventually leverage accumulates in the economy. As leverage accumulates, balance sheets gradually begin to deteriorate, and eventually excessive short-term borrowing leads to an investor-imposed liquidity squeeze, and a recession ensues. (Business cycles driven by credit-related disturbances will be referred to as "credit–induced cycles" or "credit cycles.")

The first nine business cycles of the postwar period were inflation cycles, and each was associated with the failure of a small number of financial institutions—typically commercial banks. Over time, however, these financial debacles became more complex and involved more than one type of financial institution. Liquidity disruptions eventually began to disrupt banking-related markets, and stretched overseas. The risk of contagion first became evident as far back as 1974 with the failure of Franklin National Bank, but the shift from symptomatic to systemic crises only began to show in the 1990s with the collapse of the savings and loan industry. The fundamental nature of this shift became even more evident in the 2001 corporate malfeasance recession. A forced balance sheet restructuring of the nonfinancial corporate sector set the stage for the collapse of the Dot-Com Bubble, and recession was brought about by a collapse in corporate investment spending, and a disruption in the commercial paper market.

The thrift crisis and the corporate balance sheet restructuring recessions were the credit cycle's prelude to the subprime crisis at the heart of the Great Recession. This deep and long contraction was triggered by rising default rates on the more esoteric mortgage-related products generated during the housing bubble. When the bubble burst, the collapse of the household sector's balance sheet led to the failure of a number of financial institutions, both domestically and internationally. The result was an unprecedented collapse in liquidity for the housing sector, and a recession rivaled only by that of the Great Depression. The 2007–2009 recession was followed by an uncertain and shallow recovery, as both the household sector and the banking industry needed to restructure before liquidity could flow through the economy, and stimulate demand for goods and services.

The evolution from inflation-induced to credit-induced business cycles was clearly related to the movement from a world of excess demand to that of excess supply, but it also appears to be the natural result of rising return expectations and the associated increase in risk undertaken by financial institutions. The disinflation/deflation pressures generated by an excess supply of tradable goods and commodities made the earning of double-digit returns much more difficult, forcing a shift down the credit curve by banks and investors that resulted in a business cycle that was inevitably the result of excessive risk-taking. This evolution from symptomatic to systemic financial debacles is critical to understand when assessing the likely cause of future business cycles. To this end, the following will detail the nature of all eleven postwar business cycles, and the associated financial developments that were either the result of a recession or were the cause of a downturn in the economy.

What Is a Business Cycle?

What is a recession? A recession is a significant decline in economic activity, spread across the economy—lasting more than a few months, normally visible in real GDP, real income, employment, industrial production, and wholesales or retail sales. According to the National Bureau of Economic Research (NBER), a recession begins just after the economy reaches a peak in activity, and ends as the economy reaches its trough. Between the trough and peak, the economy is in expansion. In choosing business cycle turning points, the NBER places particular emphasis on real personal income, less transfer payments, such as Social Security, and employment. These two monthly indicators measure activity across the broad economy, while industrial production and the monthly measures of sales at all levels of the production/distribution chain principally reflect manufacturing. The NBER Business Cycle Dating Committee—the arbiter of business cycle dating—also looks at a host of other indicators in forming its decisions on business cycle turning points.

The NBER prefers to wait for sufficient data before determining turning points, rather than rushing into a decision. This creates a significant lag in the process of dating the cycle turning points. The lag has led economists to view a recession as two consecutive quarterly declines in real GDP, as an alternative to the NBER's approach in calling the beginning of a recession. However, it should be noted that this process does align precisely with the official business cycle turning points determined by the NBER.

Depressions are deeper and last longer than a recession. For example, the Great Depression of the 1930s resulted in a decline in real GDP in excess of 10 percent, and a jobless rate that briefly touched 25 percent. More recently, economists have added another subcategory to contractions—a Great Recession. This is a consolidation that is deeper and longer than a recession, but not as bad as a depression. The 2007–2009 recession lasted eighteen months, and resulted in a 4.2 percent peak-to-trough decline in real GDP. A drop of 6.3 percent in employment and a 17.1 percent tumble in industrial production exceeded the comparable measure in each of the previous ten postwar business cycles, but also fell far short of the comparable measures available for the 1930s decline.

The next natural question to address is, what causes a recession? History suggests that several factors can be identified as causing a broad-based decline in economic activity. A tightening in monetary policy is a common cause of postwar

NBER Business Cycle Reference Dates, 1948–2009

		Duration in Months			
Peak	Trough	Contraction	Expansion	Cycle	
Quarterly Dates Are in Parentheses		Peak to Trough	Previous Trough to This Peak	Trough from Previous Trough	Peak from Previous Peak
November 1948 (IV)	October 1949 (IV)	11	37	48	45
July 1953 (II)	May 1954 (II)	10	45	55	56
August 1957 (III)	April 1958 (II)	8	39	47	49
April 1960 (II)	February 1961 (I)	10	24	34	32
December 1969 (IV)	November 1970 (IV)	11	106	117	116
November 1973 (IV)	March 1975 (I)	16	36	52	47
January 1980 (I)	July 1980 (III)	6	58	64	74
July 1981 (III)	November 1982 (IV)	16	12	28	18
July 1990 (III)	March 1991 (I)	8	92	100	108
March 2001 (I)	November 2001 (IV)	8	120	128	128
December 2007 (IV)	June 2009 (II)	18	73	91	81
Average, all cycles:					
1854–2009 (33 cycles)		17.5	38.7	56.2	56.4*
1854–1919 (16 cycles)		21.6	26.6	48.2	48.9**
1919–1945 (6 cycles)		18.2	35	53.2	53
1945–2009 (11 cycles)		11.1	58.4	69.5	68.5

* 32 cycles
** 15 cycles

Source: National Bureau of Economic Research

business cycles. Inflation concerns brought about by excess demand (a supply shock) has tended to motivate the Federal Reserve to constrict credit by hiking short-term rates. Energy price shocks are a prime example of a supply shock that has influenced Fed policymakers' decisions. Fiscal policy has contributed to either higher or lower inflation by stimulating or reducing excess demand through either tax policy or defense spending, or both. Government spending on social programs has tended to grow over time, with one significant inflection point during the Johnson-era Great Society experiment (see Chapter 5). Besides policy mistakes or unintended consequences of policy shifts, a collapse in confidence or a loss in wealth can also result in a recession. Additionally, deterioration in credit quality has also triggered a reduction in liquidity, resulting in a collapse in economic activity. The seeds of the Great Recession can be traced back to the July 2007 collapse of two hedge funds owned by Bear Stearns, a result of their investment in collateralized debt obligations (CDOs), which were later downgraded by Moody's and Standard & Poor's (S&P), and wiped out their capital. This event weakened the investment bank, and ultimately led to its distress sale to JPMorgan Chase & Co.

Economists have tended to divide the history of business cycles into two groups: those that occurred prior to World War II and those that occurred in the past seventy years. The significant shift in the role the US economy played in the global economy after the war—and the restructuring of the economy itself to reflect this new status—renders a somewhat meaningless comparison to the recessions prior to 1948. It could be argued that the recent rise of China as a global macro power may result in another break in the history of business cycles, but for now, this analysis will concentrate on the last eleven cycles.

Chapter 1

The 1948–1949 First
Postwar Recession

The end of postwar wage and price controls in mid-1946, and the backlog of demand for goods and services created by World War II, produced a spike in inflation. Policymakers relied on a new Keynesian style of government–intervention to dial back inflation and the fears that it would become entrenched. The political realities, however, led to a pro-cyclical tax cut instead of a revenue-neutral rebalancing of the tax burden. This forced the Fed to implement credit controls because its interest rate tools were still focused on keeping the government's interest expense as low as possible. Credit controls proved to be a blunt instrument, and the reduction in demand produced an inventory liquidation cycle, and the recession.

World War II ended on September 2, 1945, and the economy was vastly different from the Depression-era days that preceded US involvement in the conflict. Domestic manufacturing had expanded dramatically, labor unions had become well entrenched in key industries, and the US emerged from the war as a superpower. The 1948–1949 recession was technically not the first downturn to follow the war, but it was the first real test of the new political economy—or the government's ability to fulfill its obligations under the Employment Act of 1946. This seminal legislation obliged the federal government to seek to maintain "maximum employment, production, and purchasing power." The short February to October 1945 downturn was the result of the conversion from military to civilian production. The November 1948–October 1949 recession was the first test of the government's new built-in stabilizers—passed as part of the New Deal—as well as its ability to manipulate fiscal and monetary policy to counteract the adverse effects of the downturn. There was a fear, heading into the recession, that the boom of the postwar period would be followed by a return to the prewar depression once the pent-up demand had been satisfied.

Fiscal policy is one of two major levers that can be used to stimulate or constrain economic growth in order to smooth out the business cycle. Unlike monetary policy, which is the lever that can be manipulated by the Federal Reserve, fiscal policy is controlled by Congress. By decreasing taxes or increasing government spending, Congress can indirectly boost real GDP. Lowering taxes boosts consumer and corporate spending on goods and services, resulting in rising disposable income. Gains in income tend to lead to increased spending on goods and services. Increasing government procurement directly increases demand for goods and services in the economy, and in the process, also increases income generated in the economy, which leads to a second round of increased spending. Increasing taxes and cutting government spending has the exact opposite effect on the economy.

Monetary policy, on the other hand, refers to the central bank's ability to influence the level of short-term rates, which can be used to either reduce or increase the cost of borrowing by households and corporations. A lower borrowing cost tends to boost spending, whereas higher short rates tend to constrain spending by hiking the cost of financing. Keynesianism is a branch of economic theory that emphasizes the use of fiscal policy as a means of smoothing out the cyclical ups and downs that naturally occur in the economy. The manipulation of short-term interest rates and the supply of liquid assets in the economy is referred to as monetarism.

The memory of the Great Depression ran deep, and there were broad-based concerns that once the backlogged demand for construction and durables that had been created by the war was satisfied, a normal level of demand in the economy would be insufficient to maintain full employment, without massive government programs to absorb the excess supply. The mildness of the recession was subsequently seen as proof that the new elements of long-term strength had been built into the economy in the late 1930s and early 1940s. The 1948–1949 recession experience resulted in a psychological shift among economists that long-run prosperity would now be inherent, and that inflationary-driven business cycles had not been eliminated, but the magnitude had been dampened on the downswing.

What kind of recession was it? The consensus is that it was a simple inventory/inflation cycle. In response to the lack of goods available during the war, household savings expanded and provided the primary source of funding that the government needed to expand its purchases of military equipment and supplies. The return to a more normal savings rate in the postwar period fueled a boom in household demand for cars, vacuum cleaners, refrigerators, washing machines, and radios. Returning GIs got married and quickly began to have families, creating a backlog in housing. This surge in demand led to a greater need for expanded manufacturing and transportation facilities. These investments were paid for by the accumulated profits that companies had earned during the war. It is esti-mated that the postwar investment cycle peaked in 1946–1947 at 33 percent above the prewar top in 1941. Following the end of wartime price controls in mid-1946, consumer prices surged from 2.3 percent to a 14.4 percent annualized rate in 1947.

The domestic pressures on inflation were amplified by the increased Cold War tensions and the demands created by the European Economic Recovery Plan. The resulting spike in inflation was broad-based, and was quickly seen as a major economic imbalance that had to be addressed at the national level, given the new interventionist/Keynesian view of fiscal policy. In his economic report to Congress, released in January 1948, President Truman highlighted the problem of inflation and the need to establish policies that would increase production to satisfy increased household and business demand for goods and services. Seven recommendations were made, but not all were implemented. The president requested that Congress do the following:

1. Decrease taxes on individuals, and increase taxes on corporations, to maintain a budget surplus.

2. Provide the Federal Reserve with the authority to regulate consumer credit.

3. Allow the Federal Reserve to increase reserve requirements.

4. Provide the president with the authority to institute price controls on both commodities and manufactured goods to limit excessive price hikes caused by shortages.

5. Give the president legislative authority to prevent wage hikes when necessary to maintain a price ceiling.

6. Request voluntary restraints by households for scarce products.

7. Request voluntary restraints by businesses in holding the line on prices, or reducing them where possible, and request restraints by labor unions in moderating wage demands.

THE REVENUE ACT OF 1948

The Revenue Act of 1948 was vetoed by President Truman because it failed to maintain a budget surplus, which was seen as necessary to help control inflation. Congress overrode Truman's veto by a two-thirds margin in each house, and the tax cut became law. The reduction in individual taxes is seen as one of the reasons that the 1948–1949 recession proved to be relatively short and shallow. The Revenue Act reduced individual tax rates by 5 percent, to 13 percent, increased the personal exemption from $500 to $600, permitted married couples to split their income for tax purposes, and made the distinction between community property jurisdictions and non-community property jurisdictions. The Revenue Act also provided additional exemptions for taxpayers age sixty-five and over.

1947 Top Federal Tax Rates	1948 Top Federal Tax Rates
Top Rate on Regular Income: 86.5%	Top Rate on Regular Income: 82.13%
Top Rate on Capital Gains: 25%	Top Rate on Capital Gains: 25%
Top Rate on Corporate Tax: 38%	Top Rate on Corporate Tax: 38%

Congress reacted to Truman's requests by deferring spending on many public works projects, and opted to cut individual taxes, but not increase corporate taxes. In essence, fiscal policy became pro-cyclical instead of remaining neutral. The anticipated shift from a budget surplus to a deficit prompted the president to veto this legislation. Congress, however, overrode his veto, and the net reduction in taxes ultimately became an important factor in limiting the depth of the recession, but amplified the underlying inflation bias in the economy. Congress did pass legislation giving the Federal Reserve authority to regulate consumer credit and raise commercial bank reserve requirements. The president was never given the authority to ration goods or to control wages and prices.

The Federal Reserve's policy of keeping short-term interest rates low, in order to limit the effect on the government's net interest expense that had been established during the war, continued until 1951. This limited the negative effect that rising market rates had on the economy, prompting the Federal Reserve to use other tools to fight inflation. In January, and again in August of 1948, the Federal Reserve raised the discount rate—the rate at which banks borrow from the Fed—and also raised reserve requirements. Neither of these two monetary policy tools appears to have done much to slow the economy, as banks simply sold some of their large portfolios of Treasury securities accumulated during the war, to fund additional lending. However, the decision to reimpose credit controls appears to have resulted in a sharp cut in household spending, and prompted an inventory liquidation cycle. The makers of domestic monetary policy imposed minimum down payments on new loans, and maximum maturities on installment loans, in an effort to dampen demand and rein in inflation.

Quarterly Changes in Gross National Product—
First Quarter 1947 to Second Quarter 1950
(Annual Rate in Billions of Dollars, Seasonally Adjusted)

Year and Quarter	GDP Change from Preceding Quarter	
	Including Inventory Changes	Excluding Inventory Changes
1947		
Q1	+3.6	+6.6
Q2	+7.7	+7.3
Q3	1.4	+4.9
Q4	+11.2	+7.3
1948		
Q1	+3.9	+2.0
Q2	+9.6	+7.3
Q3	+5.4	+4.2
Q4	+4.0	+3.5
1949		
Q1	-6.4	-0.4
Q2	-2.0	+2.2
Q3	-1.7	-2.3
Q4	-0.1	+2.7
1950		
Q1	+8.2	+1.1
Q2	+15.3	+7.7

Source: Department of Commerce data, Benjamin Caplin, A Case Study: The 1948–1949 Recession, 1956

Credit controls proved to be very effective in limiting the demand for consumer durable goods. Specifically, consumer spending on durable goods reported on a real-time basis, from the final quarter of 1947 to the final three months of 1948, was exceptionally volatile, ranging from minus 12 percent to 25 percent. The 12 percent decline in durable goods spending recorded in the first quarter was followed by gains of 18 percent and 25 percent, respectively, in the second and third quarters, before declining again by 11 percent in the final three months of the year. Because these data are nominal, the underlying inflation bias understates the weakness in demand caused by the reduction in the postwar backlog of demand, the slowdown in marriages and births, the rising interest rate environment, and the imposition of credit controls late in the year. This dynamic caused an undesired accumulation in business inventories in 1948 that companies were forced to liquidate in 1949.

In addition to the decline in purchasing of consumer durable goods that followed the imposition of credit controls in September 1948, a decline in construction spending also played a key role in the downturn. The number of new homes started by builders is reported to have declined on a monthly basis from June to December 1948. This reduction in building clearly amplified the swing in consumer durable goods and the need for an inventory adjustment in 1949. Residential construction, in fact, was basically flat in 1949 and did not recover until the following year. Credit controls do not appear to have played a part in the consolidation in housing; instead, demographic factors, and the fact that backlogged demand had been largely satisfied, appear to have been the key factors involved.

Changes in Gross National Product, Selected Quarters, 1948–1950
(Billions of Dollars, Annual Rates, Seasonally Adjusted)

Component	Fourth Quarter 1948	Fourth Quarter 1949	Second Quarter 1950	Change from 1948 Q4 to 1949 Q4	Change from 1949 Q4 to 1950 Q2
Gross National Product	267.0	256.8	280.3	-10.2	+23.5
Personal consumption	179.8	183.0	189.7	+3.2	+6.7
Durable goods	22.5	25.0	26.8	-2.5	+1.8
Nondurable goods	101.4	99.1	100.7	-2.3	+1.6
Services	55.9	58.9	62.2	+3.0	+3.3
Gross private investment	45.7	31.0	52.0	-14.7	+21.0
New construction	17.8	18.2	22.0	+0.4	+3.8
Producers' durables	20.7	18.2	21.7	-2.5	+3.5
Change in business inventories	7.2	-5.4	8.3	-12.6	+13.7
Nonfarm only	5.6	-4.2	7.3	-9.8	+11.5
Net foreign investment	1.2	-0.5	-1.6	-1.7	-1.1
Government purchases of goods & services	40.3	43.3	40.3	+3.0	-3.0
Federal	23.6	24.5	20.7	+0.9	-3.8
State and local	16.7	18.8	19.5	+2.1	+0.7

Source: Benjamin Caplin, A Case Study: The 1948–1949 Recession, 1956

Chapter 2

The 1953–1954 Post–Korean War Recession

The rapid mobilization for the Korean War effort, and fears of the type of controls implemented during World War II, resulted in a spike in inflation in 1950. President Truman subsequently implemented wage and price controls in 1951 to dampen inflation pressures. Price controls were lifted in 1952, and wage controls were removed a year later. The Federal Reserve also tightened monetary policy in 1952, to curb inflation. Interest rates were kept higher than necessary, due to policymakers' concerns that inflation would prove to be stubborn, and the result was a sharp contraction in economic demand. The end of the Treasury-Fed Accord, which had been in place since 1941, and had kept rates artificially low, also became a factor in the recession, as the Fed strived to reassert its independence.

The second postwar recession started in July 1953 and ended in May 1954. The recession can be explained as a result of two important factors: first, the Korean War, which began in June 1950, and lasted three years until the July 1953 armistice, and second, the 1951 decision by the Federal Reserve and the Treasury to end their 1941 accord, which had the central bank keep short-term rates artificially low to reduce the government cost of funding the war effort. These two factors set the stage for a spike in inflation, and a monetary policy response that pushed the economy into a relatively short, ten-month downturn.

The Korean War was the first surrogate war of the Cold War period, and it caught the United States with a very low level of national defense spending. The unexpected nature of the attack by North Korea on South Korea resulted in a rapid mobilization effort that taxed the domestic economy's ability to come to the aid of its ally. Even after much massaging of the data during the intervening years, the effect of the war effort is still evident in the national income data. Annual defense spending, and its share of GDP, increased substantially in 1951 and 1952, as deliveries of defense-related equipment, ordered in 1950, began to leave defense and civilian factories. Defense spending surged to $52 billion in 1953, from $19.3 billion in 1950. As a share of the economy, national defense spending increased to 14.2 percent from 6.5 percent over the same four-year period. Defense spending remained virtually unchanged in 1954, even though the conflict ended halfway through the year.

The surprise attack on South Korea by North Korea reignited fears in the United States of the rationing implemented during World War II, and as a result, households rushed to buy consumer durables. Everything from cars to televisions was in hot demand, and businesses rushed to buy building

Nominal Defense Spending and Share of GNP 1949–1953, Annual Data

Period	Total Gross National Product	National Security*	% GNP
1949	257.3	19.3	7.5
1950	285.1	18.5	6.5
1951	328.2	37.3	11.4
1952	346.1	48.5	14.0
1953	364.9	52.0	14.2

*"National security" expenditures include the items classified as such in The Budget of the United States Government for the Fiscal Year ending June 30, 1954

Source: Economic Report of the President, 1955

materials and order equipment that they expected would soon be in short supply, as production was diverted from civilian to military use. Prices were built up in the process, and inflation spiked. Unions demanded increased wages to maintain worker purchasing power. Increased demand for workers also bid up wages as young men were drafted into service to supplement the South Korean army, as Chinese soldiers added to the ranks of the North. As such, marginally attached workers had to be pulled back into the labor force with higher wages. This macro dynamic was quickly reflected in the consumer price index (CPI), and in average hourly earnings. Real-time data show that the CPI surged by almost 8 percent in 1951 after having increased by only 1 percent the year before. Policy actions taken by the Truman team quickly brought prices under control—the CPI rose by just 2.25 percent in 1952 and by 0.8 percent in 1953. However, the same cannot be said for hourly earnings that rose by 8.5 percent in 1951, and by an additional 5 percent and 6 percent in each of the following two years, respectively. As such, wage increases outpaced price increases during the Korean War.

The early spike in consumer prices prompted quick action by the Truman administration, which instituted price and wage controls in January 1951. Price controls for many products were removed in 1952, while some wage controls remained in place until early 1953, and all price controls were finally lifted that October. The administration also placed controls on the allocation of critical materials needed for the war effort, but these were partially lifted in 1952 and completely lifted in June 1953.

To fund the war effort and to help curb inflation, Congress passed three separate tax bills between 1950 and 1951, which raised taxes paid by both individuals and corporations. These three legislative initiatives had a significant effect on personal taxes paid by households. Specifically, in 1950, personal taxes totaled $20.9 billion, and by 1951 these tax payments had gone up to $29.3 billion, for a 40 percent jump. Tax payments continued to rise in 1951 to $34.4 billion, another 17.7 percent, before topping out at $36 billion in 1953. Taxes paid by corporations also rose sharply during this period but were much more frontloaded. Corporate tax payments spiked by almost 53 percent

Average Gross Hourly Earnings in Manufacturing VS CPI All Items

Period	Manufacturing Hourly Earnings	Year on Year Change	CPI All Items	Year on Year Change
1929	$0.566		73.3	
1930	$0.552	-2%	71.4	-3%
1931	$0.515	-7%	65.0	-9%
1932	$0.446	-13%	58.4	-10%
1933	$0.442	-1%	55.3	-5%
1934	$0.532	20%	57.2	3%
1935	$0.550	3%	58.7	3%
1936	$0.556	1%	59.3	1%
1937	$0.624	12%	61.4	4%
1938	$0.627	0%	60.3	-2%
1939	$0.633	1%	59.4	-1%
1940	$0.661	4%	59.9	1%
1941	$0.729	10%	62.9	5%
1942	$0.853	17%	69.7	11%
1943	$0.961	13%	74.0	6%
1944	$1.019	6%	75.2	2%
1945	$1.023	0%	76.9	2%
1946	$1.086	6%	83.4	8%
1947	$1.237	14%	95.5	15%
1948	$1.350	9%	102.8	8%
1949	$1.401	4%	101.8	-1%
1950	$1.465	5%	102.8	1%
1951	$1.590	9%	111.0	8%
1952	$1.670	5%	113.5	2%
1953	$1.770	6%	114.4	1%
1954	$1.810	2%	114.9	0%

Source: Economic Report of the President, 1955

in 1950 but then topped out before receding in 1954, as the temporary hike enacted for the war was allowed to expire after hostilities ceased.

The Revenue Tax Act of 1950 reduced prior tax cuts that were enacted just before the outbreak of hostilities on the Korean peninsula. Under this legislation, individual tax rates would be tentatively reduced by 13 percent instead of 17 percent on the first $400 of income. Between $400 and $100,000 of taxable income, the marginal rate was temporarily reduced by 8 percent instead of 12 percent, and for income in excess of $100,000, the marginal rate was reduced by 7.3 percent instead of 9.75 percent. For corporations, the 1950 act eliminated the graduated structure of normal income and surcharge tax rates with a flat tax of 25 percent on normal income, and a 20 percent surcharge tax rate on net income over $25,000.

An excess profit tax was also implemented in 1950. Excess profits were seen as profits attributable to excess government spending due to the war, and higher prices paid for goods by households due to wartime-induced shortages. The Excess Profit Tax Act of 1950 levied an additional 2 percent tax on corporate income. The final tax hike executed for the war effort was the Revenue Act of 1951. This legislation temporarily increased individual income tax rates through the end of 1953 and temporarily increased corporate tax rates by 5 percent through March 31,

1954. Individual tax rates were increased by either 11 percent of the normal tax rate or 8 percent of surtax on net income.

Individual and Corporate Tax Payments

	Billions of Dollars	
	Personal Taxes	Corporate Tax Liability
1929	2.6	1.4
1930	2.5	0.8
1931	1.9	0.5
1932	1.5	0.4
1933	1.5	0.5
1934	1.6	0.7
1935	1.9	1.0
1936	2.3	1.4
1937	2.9	1.5
1938	2.9	1.0
1939	2.4	1.4
1940	2.6	2.8
1941	3.3	7.6
1942	6.0	11.4
1943	17.8	14.1
1944	18.9	12.9
1945	20.9	10.7
1946	18.8	9.1
1947	21.5	11.3
1948	21.1	12.5

continued

1949	18.7	10.4
1950	20.9	17.8
1951	29.3	22.5
1952	34.4	20.0
1953	36.0	21.1
1954	32.9	17.2

Source: Economic Report of the President, 1955

Federal Reserve policy during the 1950–1953 period contributed to the second postwar recession as policymakers responded to the spike in inflation that followed the outbreak of the Korean War. Policymakers were also concerned that inflation would reemerge once the Truman wage and price controls were lifted. By 1951, the CPI had surged by 8 percent, and had dropped to just 2.25 percent in 1952, following the administration's intervention to contain wages and prices. The decision to end the Treasury-Fed Accord in 1951 also put the Federal Reserve in a position in which policymakers wanted to reassert their independence, and markets were not accustomed to the Federal Reserve setting rates based on macro developments.

During the ten years that stretched from 1941 to 1951, the Treasury and the Federal Reserve had an accord to help the government finance the cost of World War II and the reconstruction of Europe. Under this accord, the Federal Reserve used its ability to buy Treasury debt in the open market to keep interest rates as low as possible under the economic conditions of the time. This accord limited the Fed's ability to conduct

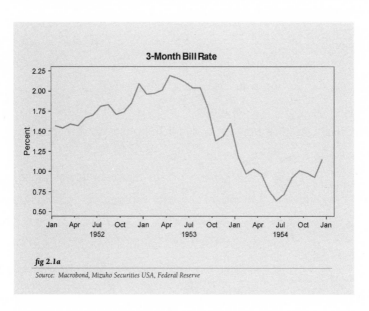

fig 2.1a

Source: Macrobond, Mizuho Securities USA, Federal Reserve

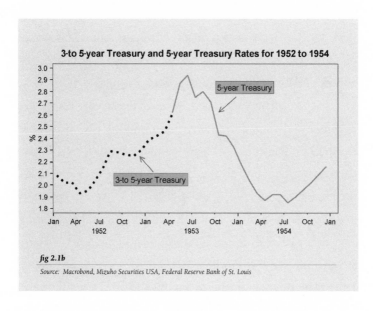

fig 2.1b

Source: Macrobond, Mizuho Securities USA, Federal Reserve Bank of St. Louis

monetary policy, and by 1951, the accord was formally terminated in response to pressure from the Fed. As such, the economic expansion that preceded the 1953–1954 recession was the first postwar cycle in which the Fed was free to set short-term rates as required to achieve its stated mandate of "maximizing employment, stabilizing prices, and moderating long-term interest rates."

The result was a general rise in interest rates along the curve. Treasury 3-month bill rates moved up sharply, reflecting a tightening in monetary policy. These 3-month bills yielded 1.57 percent in January 1952, and climbed to 2.09 percent by the end of the year. Rates continued to rise into April 1953, where they peaked at 2.19 percent before declining to about 1 percent in early 1954. The recession began in July 1953 and ended in May 1954, a fairly tight correlation with the movement in short-term rates. Longer-term rates followed a similar pattern—the yield on 3- and 5-year Treasury securities rose by almost one hundred basis points over a similar period, rising to 2.94 percent in June 1953 from 2.08 percent. Long rates also followed short rates down, dropping to 1.87 percent in April 1954. Sensing that the downdraft in inflation was sustainable as price controls were being lifted, the Federal Reserve reversed its tightening, and in June 1953, it unexpectedly lowered reserve requirements, providing a lift to the economy. The 1953–1954 recession produced just two quarters of negative Gross National Product (GNP) in 1953, and the same in 1954. The nominal economy contracted by 2.9 percent and 7.1 percent in the third and fourth quarters, respectively. The economy continued to contract in early 1954, with a 5.1 percent decline, taped to a just 0.4 percent net decline between the second and third quarter before bouncing back to a solid 6.3 percent rise in the fourth quarter.

Quarterly % Change in Real GNP

1953	Q1	4.1
	Q2	9.3
	Q3	-2.9
	Q4	-7.1
1954	Q1	-5.1
	Q2	0.2
	Q3	-0.6
	Q4	6.3

Source: Economic Report of the President, 1955

Chapter 3

The 1957–1958 Eisenhower Recession

Although relatively short in duration, at only eight months, the recession of 1957–1958 was perceived as deeper than the two prior postwar downturns, and was associated with a sharp, worldwide consolidation. The US downturn was caused by a hangover in investment spending after a boom that shortened the 1953–1954 downturn. Accelerated depreciation led to a rush of investment spending that got ahead of itself. Reduced capital investment was complemented by a post–Korean War rollback in military spending. The Federal Reserve tightened monetary policy with an anti-inflation campaign that did not deliver all expected results. The Soviet Union's launch of Sputnik on October 4, 1957, is seen as having cut the 1957–1958 recession short as the Eisenhower administration reversed course, and Cold War military spending was ramped up again. The Fed also reversed gears, and interest rates fell after having been increased to restrain inflation.

The recession that lasted from August 1957 to April 1958 has been called the Eisenhower recession. A number of the president's critics at the time claimed that an anti-inflation campaign waged by the Federal Reserve was being orchestrated to depress union wage demands. The fact that the recession did not correct the inflation bias in the economy suggests that political pressures mounted fairly quickly as the labor market slumped. The heating up of the Cold War after the Soviet Union surprised the West with its missile technology led to a sharp increase in military spending.

The eight-month downturn proved to be deep. In the six months from August 1957 to February 1958, the Federal Reserve's index of industrial production declined by more than 10 percent. Unemployment was estimated, at the time, to have risen to 5,173,000 people (an increase of about two million people) in just six months. Steel production dropped to a weekly low of 1,415,000 tons in February 1958—only 52.4 percent, for its lowest capacity usage rate that month, down from 93.5 percent a year earlier. Motor vehicle production was also slashed to a weekly low of 101,266 vehicles compared to 161,865 twelve months earlier.

The Eisenhower recession was caused by a number of factors: increased inflation pressure and the eventual tightening in monetary policy; a cut in investment spending after accelerated depreciation pulled spending forward; and a postwar reduction in fiscal policy, combined with a White House that refused to use explicit counter-cyclical fiscal policy, even as the economy lost momentum. The seeds of the 1957–1958 recession were sown in the stimulus that policymakers provided to end the prior downturn. Tax cuts for both individuals and corporations, and the end of consumer credit controls near the bottom of the 1954 cycle, resulted in a much more powerful rebound in the economy than had been anticipated in 1955. An increase in both consumer and mortgage credit stimulated the production of nearly eight million new vehicles that year, and more than 1.3 million new homes. The increase in demand resulted in a 7 percent rise in plant and equipment expenditures in 1955, and a record 22 percent increase in 1956. The increasing pressures on resources and manpower produced a 2.6 percent rise in consumer prices between January and June 1956, an acceleration of 3.1 percent during the second half of the year. This acceleration in inflation continued into the first half of 1957, and the result was a tightening in monetary policy. This translated into an exceptionally strong real GNP performance at the time. According to data available in early 1959, GNP accelerated to 4 percent in the second quarter, from 1.5 percent in the first quarter of 1957. The acceleration continued into the second half, with a 5.5 percent increase in GNP in the third quarter, and 9.8 percent in the fourth quarter. This solid expansion began to lose some momentum in 1957, with GNP coming in the first three quarters at 5.4 percent, 4.6 percent, and 4 percent, respectively. In the fourth quarter, however, real GNP dipped to 5.9 percent, followed by an 11.4 percent decline over the January to March period, before rebounding in the third quarter.

Consumer Price Index in Real Time

	Annualized Percentage Change
January–June 1955	0.2
July–December 1955	0.5
January–June 1956	2.6
July–December 1956	3.1
January–June 1957	3.8
July–December 1957	2.3

Source: BLS, US Department of Labor, 1955, 1956, 1957, 1958, Recession Prevention Handbook, Norman Frumkin, 2010

Rising inflation pressures led the Federal Reserve to tighten monetary policy in an attempt to regain control over prices as the labor market tightened. Specifically, the federal funds rate (the rate banks pay to borrow from each other) was increased by one hundred basis points in 1956, to 3.5 percent between August and October. The restraint on bank credit, however, continued until the fourth quarter of 1957. The discount rate (the rate banks pay to borrow from the Federal Reserve) was increased to 3 percent by the end of 1956, and was hiked another fifty basis points to 3.5 percent in August 1957. Longer-term rates also rose over this period. The yield on the 3- to 5-year Treasury notes were on an upward trajectory from January 1956 through October 1957, rising to 4 percent from 2.7 percent, before declining to 3 percent by year's end.

The economy also suffered from a decline in investment spending in 1957 after experiencing a slowdown in 1956. This drop-off in non-residential investment reflected not just higher rates and the expectation of a slowing in the economy, but also a payback for the acceleration in capital accumulation sponsored by the Truman administration to temper the 1953–1954 contraction. To stimulate the economy, accelerated depreciation was introduced into the IRS code in 1954: "Three principal approaches to depreciation liberalization have been urged. One is to substitute replacement cost for original cost as a basis for depreciation deduction. A second is to alter the pattern of depreciation deductions so that a larger part of the depreciable amount is charged against income in the earlier years of the asset's service life. A third is to shorten the period over which the costs of the depreciable facilities are to be charged, as depreciation, against income."

The shift from straight line to double-declining balances—a doubling of the depreciation rate—pulled investment spending forward, resulting in a shortfall of investment spending a few years further out in the calendar. According to real or constant (1947) dollar data compiled by the Commerce Department at the time, real gross private domestic investment spending accelerated to $46.6 billion in 1955 after totaling only $38.5 billion in 1953. The 21 percent spike in investment spending did not last long; in fact, real investment spending had contracted by almost 5 percent by 1957, helping to tip the economy into recession.

A final contributor to the 1957–1958 recession was the lack of counter cyclical fiscal policy or, rather, the conservative nature of the Eisenhower team. Although Eisenhower was often accused of having a balanced budget "fetish," he

Gross Private Domestic Investment (in Billions of 1947 Dollars)

Year	Billions of Dollars
1953	38.5
1954	37.9
1955	46.6
1956	47.6
1957	44.4

Source: The Eisenhower Recession, T.N. Vance, March 1958

did accept that budget deficits should increase during recessions, and shift to surpluses during expansions. As such, in the early days of his administration, military spending was cut by upward of 4 percent from a peak of 14.4 percent of the overall economy in 1952, following the signing of the armistice that ended the Korean War. In fact, estimates of the impact of fiscal policy on the economy during the Eisenhower years suggest that the policy was highly contractionary during 1953–1956, but turned stimulative during the recession years. The stimulus resulted from economic stabilizers built into the budget following the Depression and not from an explicit change in policy. According to estimates compiled in 1990, and displayed in Table 3.1, aggregate fiscal policy added a little more than $10 billion to real GNP in 1957, and increased to $15.5 billion in 1958, after having subtracted more than $30 billion from the economy over the prior three years.

Aggregate Fiscal Policy Impact Measures on Real GNP
(Billions of Dollars)

Year	Quarters				Yearly Total
	First	Second	Third	Fourth	
1953	3.885	2.811	-0.767	2.852	8.781
1954	-11.328	-8.199	-3.482	-2.177	-25.187
1955	-1.934	-3.459	2.566	-2.233	-5.059
1956	-0.400	1.360	-3.111	1.661	-0.490
1957	6.987	1.995	-1.051	2.146	10.078
1958	5.168	6.083	1.800	2.472	15.524
1959	-6.674	-1.105	-1.989	0.380	-9.388
1960	-4.927	2.162	2.375	2.524	2.134

Source: President Eisenhower, Economic Policy and the 1960 Election,
Ann Mari May, June 1990

Disaggregated estimates displayed in Table 3.3 reveal
that federal purchases of goods were highly contractionary
in 1954, and continued to be a negative contributor in 1955,
causing real GNP to decline in those years by $28.3 billion
and $2.8 billion, respectively. A reduction in military jobs
added an extra $1.5 billion and $2.2 billion to the drag on
real GDP in each of those two years. In contrast, Congress
initiated a change in excise taxes in 1954, as an anti-recession
action that the Eisenhower administration signed into law,
but only because the net effect of the cuts was offset by holding the corporate tax rate at 52 percent when it would have
fallen to 47 percent.

Disaggregated Fiscal Policy Impact Measures on Real GNP
(Yearly Totals in Billions of Dollars)

Fiscal Policy	1953	1954	1955	1956	1957	1958	1959	1960
Federal Government Purchases of Goods	8.390	-28.304	-2.819	0.013	3.701	8.381	-6.606	0.428
Personal Income Tax Rate	0.164	0.994	-0.156	-0.385	0.065	0.306	-0.328	-0.369
Profit Tax Rate	0.097	0.118	-0.059	0.074	0.028	-0.036	0.009	0.190
Indirect Business Tax Rate	0.220	0.959	-0.232	-0.518	0.681	0.064	-0.119	-0.091
Employee Social Security Tax Rate	-0.032	-0.283	-0.070	-0.114	-0.265	0.019	-0.290	-0.489
Employer Social Security Tax Rate	0.057	-0.119	-0.042	-0.024	-0.048	0.062	-0.219	-0.213
Civilian Jobs	-0.961	-0.311	0.053	0.118	-0.353	0.153	0.297	-0.020
Military Jobs	-0.174	-1.524	-2.179	-0.811	-0.618	-0.742	-0.669	0.001
Transfer Payments to Households	1.120	3.332	0.398	1.626	4.163	3.724	1.139	2.639
Grants-in-aid to State and Local Governments	0.000	0.004	-0.002	-0.001	0.000	0.011	-0.009	0.003

Source: President Eisenhower, Economic Policy and the 1960 Election,
Ann Mari May, June 1990

Chapter 4

The 1960–1961 Rolling Adjustment Recession

The April 1960–February 1961 recession is known as the rolling recession because major industries got caught up in the downturn, at different times. The recession is also known for having been preceded by a short two-year expansion, and was followed by a long 106-month expansion. The downturn was primarily the result of the Federal Reserve's inflation concerns that resulted in an inventory correction that dominated the decline in real GDP.

The fourth recession of the postwar period was known at the time for having been preceded by the shortest expansion. The April 1958–April 1960 expansion lasted only two years, but even more interesting is the fact that the expansion which followed the February 1961 trough lasted 106 months (eight years and ten months). The cause of the 1960–1961 recession was monetary policy tightening in response to a perceived inflation bias caused by a sharp rebound in the economy following the end of the steel strike in November 1959. This inflation concern prompted a fairly aggressive monetary policy tightening, and resulted in a short and sharp inventory correction. The recession, which lasted ten months, was cut short by a rapid Fed easing of policy, the heating up of the Cold War, and acceleration in government spending on large-scale projects, such as the interstate highway system.

Although the recession began in April 1960, employment, production, and income that year reached levels well above those attained in 1959. The upswing in the economy was concentrated in the first half of 1959, with unemployment rising and production declining in the second half. For the year, real GNP increased by 2.6 percent. The upturn in the economy during the first half of 1960 continued the turnaround that began in the spring of 1958. The post 1957–1958 expansion was aided by the shallowness of the recession. Consumer spending and income had begun to rise in the middle of 1958, and is a key reason that the recession lasted only eight months, and never really wrung inflationary pressures out of the economy in the Fed's interpretation of the business cycle dynamics. This early upturn in income and spending cut short the inventory correction at the heart of the late 1950s recession. Additional upward momentum in 1958 came from an increase in residential construction and by investment in plant and equipment. The Soviet Union's launch of the Sputnik satellite in late 1957 led to increased government spending in 1958, and when combined with easier monetary policy, the recovery from the recession proved to be fairly robust.

The expansion of April 1958 to April 1960 continued to build momentum in 1959, although a steel strike provided a key disruption. In early 1959, the economy began to accelerate in anticipation of a steel strike, and a buildup in inventory to avoid possible delivery delays. The long strike that dominated developments during the second half of the year liquidated these excess inventories, leading to a drop in both employment and income. As a result, final demand GDP, less inventory accumulation, slowed from an average of 9.2 percent in the first six months of the year to just 2.7 percent over the final two quarters of the year, with October to December final demand rising by just 0.2 percent. Although sharp, this drop in final demand was less dramatic than had been expected.

The steel strike ended in November 1959 after a federal court issued an injunction that resulted in a sharp rebound in economic activity. Real GNP surged by 11.4 percent in the first quarter of 1960, while final demand snapped back by 14.9 percent. Steel users rushed to rebuild depleted stocks, and automobile manufacturers ramped up production. This sharp rebound led to widespread speculation of a boom, and with it, fears of growing inflation pressures. As 1960 progressed, stockpiles returned to normal levels, and the high rate of replacement demand slowed, as did an economy that expanded by 5.3 percent in the second quarter. Expenditures on fixed investment, consumption, and net exports all contributed to a 9.8 percent rise in final demand during the same three-month period. In the second half of the year, expenditures on plant and equipment accelerated as final sales expanded by 3.9 percent on average. A 4 percent drag from inventory liquidation, however, pulled the economy into the 1960–1961 recession.

Gross National Product, 1958–60
[Billions of Dollars, Seasonally Adjusted Annual Rates]

Period Total		Gross National Product			Change in Gross National Product from Preceding Quarter		
		Final Purchases	Change in Business Inventories	Total	Final Purchases	Change in Business Inventories	
1958:	Q1	432.0	438.9	-6.9	-10.3	-4.6	-5.7
	Q2	436.8	441.3	-4.5	4.8	2.4	2.4
	Q3	447.0	448.6	-1.6	10.2	7.3	2.9
	Q4	461.0	458.1	2.9	14.0	9.5	4.5
1959:	Q1	473.1	465.5	7.6	12.1	7.4	4.7
	Q2	487.9	476.4	11.5	14.8	10.9	3.9
	Q3	481.4	481.5	-0.1	-6.5	5.1	-11.6
	Q4	486.4	481.7	4.7	5.0	0.2	4.8
1960:	Q1	501.3	489.9	11.4	14.9	8.2	6.7
	Q2	505.0	499.7	5.3	3.7	9.8	-6.1
	Q3	503.5	502.9	0.6	-1.5	3.2	-4.7
	Q4	503.5	507.5	-4.0	0.0	4.6	-4.6

Source: Department of Commerce

Changes in Consumer Price Index, 1959 and 1960

		Percentage Change	
Item	Relative Importance December 1959 (Percent)	Dec. 1958 to Nov. 1959	Dec. 1959 to Nov. 1960
All Items	100.0	1.5	1.5
Commodities	64.1	0.8	1.0
Food	28.0	-0.7	2.8
Food at home	23.2	-1.5	3.0
Commodities less food	36.1	1.8	-0.4
Nondurable commodities	22.5	2.4	1.0
Apparel	8.9	1.7	1.4
Shoes	1.4	7.4	0.1
Durable commodities	13.6	1.1	-2.7
Cars, new	3.0	0.5	-2.9
Cars, used	1.8	6.4	-14.2
Durables less cars	8.8	0.2	-0.5
Appliances	3.1	0.2	-1.1
Services	35.9	2.9	2.4
Rent	6.2	1.3	1.3
All services less rent	29.7	3.1	2.6

Source: Department of Labor

Prices in different economic sectors followed divergent trends in 1960, whereas, in 1959, price trends tended to be very similar across sectors. Prices of consumer durables and nondurables rose in 1959 by 1.1 percent and 2.4 percent, respectively, resulting in a 1.5 percent rise in headline consumer prices. For 1960, these two major contributors to headline inflation diverged sharply, falling by 2.7 percent and rising by 1 percent, respectively, with the headline increasing at the same 1.5 percent rate.

This divergence reflected a slackening of demand and a restocking of durable goods supplies as the year progressed. The gain in nondurable goods prices in 1960 resulted from a sharp rise in farm prices and in processed foods, while industrial prices drifted lower. This weakening in durable goods prices reflected a combination of monetary and fiscal policy designed to avoid speculative excesses, and limit the effect of capacity constraints on prices. The result was a slowdown in wage inflation. Average hourly earnings of production workers in manufacturing, which had been rising at more than 5 percent in 1956 and 1957, rose by only 3.4 percent in 1959. However, this increase exceeded the gains in productivity over the previous decade, and policymakers felt required to respond.

The run-up in inflation prior to the onset of the recession was not that high, but the Fed was concerned that the shallow 1957–1958 recession left the economy vulnerable to an unexpectedly large acceleration in inflation as capacity constraints loomed. To preempt such a development, the Fed hiked the funds rate from 2.5 percent in January–February 1959 to a high

Net Changes in Commercial Bank Holdings of
Loans and Investments, 1955–60 [Billions of Dollars]

Loans and investments	1955	1956	1957	1958	1959 (1)	1960 (2)
Loans (excluding interbank) and investments (3)	4.6	4.2	4.9	15.1	4.0	8.4
Loans (excluding interbank) (3)	11.6	7.6	3.5	4.3	11.9	5.8
Business	6.4	5.5	1.8	-0.1	5.1 (4)	2.2 (5)
Real estate	2.4	1.7	0.6	2.1	2.5	0.7
Consumer	2.3	1.4	1.2	0.2	2.8	1.4
Security	0.6	-0.8	-0.1	0.4	0.2	0.2
Agricultural	-0.7	-0.3	-0.1	0.9	N/A (6)	0.7
Nonbank financial institutions	N/A (7)	N/A (7)	N/A (7)	N/A (7)	N/A (7)	-0.1
All other	0.9	0.4	0.3	1.0	1.5	0.6
Investments	-7.0	-3.5	1.3	10.8	-7.9	2.7
U.S. Government securities	-7.4	-3.0	-0.3	8.1	-7.7	2.4
Other securities	0.4	-0.4	1.7	2.6	-0.2	0.3

(1) Structural changes in 1959 are excluded.
(2) Preliminary estimates by Council of Economic Advisers
(3) Total loans are net of, and individual loans are gross of, valuation reserves.
(4) Includes estimate of loans to nonbank financial institutions on December 31, 1959
(5) Excludes loans to nonbank financial institutions, shown separately, and is not strictly comparable with previous data
(6) Less than $50 million
(7) Reported in business and "all other" loans prior to June 10, 1959, and estimated in business and "all other" loans on December 31, 1959

Source: Board of Governors of the Federal Reserve System

of 4 percent from October to December of that same year. The yield on 3- to 5-year Treasury notes increased from 3.9 percent between January and March 1959 to a high of 4.95 percent that December. As the jobless rate climbed to a high of 7.1 percent and the economy slumped, the Fed began to reverse policy. By November 1960, the funds rate had been cut by 1.5 percent, and by December, the 3- to 5-year Treasury rate had dipped to 3.5 percent, setting the stage for the recovery that began the following February. To complement the easing in interest rates, the Fed also eased reserve requirements as loan demand slowed in 1960. Specifically, required reserves against demand deposits were eased in two steps between September and December. Central city banks saw their required reserves cut to 16.5 percent in September, from 18 percent, while rural banks' reserve requirements were increased from 11 percent to 12 percent as a partial offset. The Fed also expanded nonborrowed reserves by $7.1 billion in 1960 in an attempt to stimulate lending to get the economy moving.

Policymakers also faced a balance of payments problem in 1960–1961. In 1960, the surplus of American net exports of goods and service began to increase. This improvement, unfortunately, was due to a decline in imports as the recession took hold. In 1961, the net export surplus had increased to $5.2 billion. In contrast, the deficit in financial transactions was much larger in both 1960 and 1961 than in earlier years because of greatly increased short-term capital outflows. The balance of payments deficit in 1960 was settled with a $1.7 billion outflow of gold, and a $2.2 billion increase in debt liabilities owed to overseas investors. The balance of payments deficit narrowed somewhat in 1961, but $820 million in gold still flowed overseas, and foreigners bought another $1.7 billion in short-term domestic liabilities. This outflow of gold and increased foreign ownership of debt was a concern to policymakers, who were no longer worried about protecting the dollar from further erosion from inflation, as the economy had slipped into a recession. There was a need, however, to protect the dollar from rapid appreciation. As such, the Fed's shift to an accommodative stance was also supported by the balance of payments developments and the outflow of gold.

The economy also became a central issue in the 1960 presidential election that pitted Vice President Richard Nixon against the Democratic nominee, Senator John F. Kennedy. Unfortunately for the Nixon team, President Eisenhower was conservative in his approach to the downturn, while Kennedy was advancing an aggressive agenda of increasing government spending, cutting taxes, and increasing funding for education. The stark contrast between these two alternatives helped lead to Kennedy's victory, and would set the stage for an expansion that would extend for almost nine years.

Chapter 5

The 1969–1970 Nixon Recession

The fifth postwar recession followed on the back of the longest postwar expansion which lasted 106 months, from trough to peak. The expansion was dominated by fundamental changes in the structure of the economy as the Cold War expanded geographically and off planet, and the Great Society experiment increased the government's involvement in the day-to-day workings of the economy. Additionally, the expansion witnessed the largest private-sector bankruptcy and a strike against the country's largest manufacturing company. The fact that both fiscal and monetary policy supported the expansion increased the inflation pressures that accumulated during the period, and eventually led to the fiscal and monetary policy tightening that ultimately caused the recession, but did not fully eliminate the underlying inflation bias in the economy.

The December 1969 to November 1970 recession proved to be a turning point in the economy as excess demand increased its grip and set the stage for the great inflation. To understand how this inflation dynamic took hold, it is important to understand the geopolitical developments of the period and the far-reaching effect they had on the economy. It is also important to understand the socioeconomic changes that occurred—an expanding middle class, an unpopular war in Southeast Asia, and the social tensions surfacing in large cities. Traditional industries ran into global competition and increased environmental awareness as corporations shifted production to less densely populated areas, leaving many workers displaced by the changing reality. The power of unions to maintain and try to advance members' purchasing power accelerated this process, and resulted in a wage-price spiral that would dominate macroeconomic developments and investors' psychology for decades thereafter.

This unprecedented growth spurt was reflected in the labor market and in the overall size of the economy. The civilian jobless rate, in the run-up to the 1969–1970 recession, fell to a low of 3.3 percent recorded during 1969, from 5.5 percent in 1962. Economists at the time estimated the full employment jobless rate at 4.5 percent. These labor market gains reflected an economy that was expanding rapidly. In fact, real GNP rose by an average of 5.6 percent over the 1962–1965 period before slowing somewhat to a still solid 4.2 percent average over the next four years. This growth upswing resulted in rising inflation and wages. The uptick in consumer prices was significant by 1969 when this key metric grew by 6.1 percent from December 1968.

The key geopolitical developments that propelled the economy to a postwar record expansion can be traced back to the Soviet Union's launch of Sputnik 1 on October 4, 1957. This simple satellite circled the globe until January 4, 1958, when it burned up during reentry into the atmosphere. The technological leap forward evident in this one event touched off a space race that wouldn't peak until July 20, 1969, when astronauts from Apollo 11 touched down on the lunar surface. The investment in new technology necessary to achieve this goal created new industries and increased the demand for highly skilled workers. This fiscal stimulus affected the economy in multiple ways that extended its reach well beyond the initial investment.

Following on the back of the space race that opened a new avenue for Cold War spending, Berlin, was divided between the Soviet Union and the Allied Powers after World War II. This proved to be the next geopolitical flash point that led to increased defense spending—not just for humanitarian aid to West Berlin residents who became trapped in their half of the city during a Soviet blockade after the war, but also in advanced equipment and manpower to fight the Cold War. The massive airlift of food and supplies to West Berlin in 1948–1949 was just the tip of the iceberg. Next came the construction of the Berlin Wall, which began on August 13, 1961; it remained in place until November 1989.

A little more than one year after the Berlin Wall went up, the Kennedy administration faced off against the Soviet Union over a missile installation being established in Cuba with the help of the Communist regime of Fidel Castro. Although the missile scare lasted only thirteen days, it brought the world to the brink of nuclear war and spread the Cold War to the North American continent.

The biggest geopolitical event of the period was the escalation of the US military's involvement in the Vietnam War. Like the Korean War, this was another surrogate war waged by the Soviet Union and China against the American-dominated West.

The American military began sending advisors to South Vietnam in the 1950s, but US involvement escalated in the early part of the decade, with troop levels tripling in both 1961 and 1962. By November 1963, there were sixteen thousand military personnel in South Vietnam, up from the original nine hundred advisors sent under Eisenhower. Troop strength increased further after the Gulf of Tonkin incident in 1964, in which a US destroyer was fired upon by North Vietnamese gunboats. A contingent of 3,500 marines was deployed to South Vietnam in March 1965 to provide security for US airmen and other logistical personnel, initiating the American involvement in the ground war. By March 1965, two hundred thousand marines were stationed in South Vietnam, and by 1968, US involvement peaked at more than five hundred thousand servicemen. Public support for the war began to decline rapidly after it became clear that South Vietnamese soldiers would not be able to replace US soldiers. Even though the North's 1968 Tet Offensive failed, the near collapse of the South's defenses proved to be the turning point in domestic support for the war.

By October 1969, President Nixon had dispatched eighteen B-52 bombers to Vietnam and began to carpet-bomb the North while he slowly began removing ground troops. The bombing weakened Soviet support for the North, and jump-started the long-stalled peace talks. The Paris Peace Accords were signed in

January 1973, and the US withdrew its troops from the South. The cease-fire did not last long, and even though the South was much better supplied than the North, a series of military setbacks led to the eventual fall of Saigon in April 1975. Antiwar sentiment at home prevented then–President Ford from sending emergency supplies to the South, as had been promised by the Nixon team, when the cease-fire was signed. The scope of the American military's involvement in Vietnam was significantly positive for the economy during the build-up phase, but turned into a drag as involvement in the conflict wound down. To give an idea of the effect the run-up in military spending had during the expansion phase before the 1969–1970 recession, total defense spending increased to $80.5 billion in 1969, from $47.3 billion in 1961, and declined to $76.4 billion in 1971.

Federal Budget Outlays, National Defense, 1961–1972

Gross National Product		National Defense Spending	
Year	Percentage Change	Year	Percentage Change
1961	1.9	1961	3.2
1962	6.6	1962	7.8
1963	4.0	1963	2.3
1964	5.5	1964	2.6
1965	6.3	1965	-7.5
1966	6.5	1966	14.5
1967	2.6	1967	23.4
1968	4.7	1968	14.9
1969	2.8	1969	0.9

Source: Economic Report of the President, 1970 and 1971

Another key contributor to the extended expansion that followed the 1960–1961 recession was the Great Society experiment launched by President Johnson between 1964 and 1965. The Great Society's main goals were to eliminate poverty and racial injustice, and establish new programs to address education, medical care, urban problems, rural poverty, and transportation. Although the scope and scale of the new programs resembled those of President Franklin D. Roosevelt's New Deal agenda, the macroeconomic conditions were in stark contrast. Unlike the New Deal, which was in response to the Great Depression, the Johnson programs were advanced just as postwar prosperity had begun to fade, and the boost extended the expansion well into the end of the decade. Besides launching Medicare, Medicaid, and welfare, President Johnson also guided the Kennedy tax cut through Congress in 1964. The tax cut included an across-the-board cut in marginal rates. The top tax rate was cut by 20 percent, from 91 percent to 71 percent. The tax plan also significantly reduced marginal tax rates and lowered the buckets for corporations. The tax cut, more than the social initiatives advanced by President Johnson, received credit for the robust 106-month long expansion that preceded the 1969–1970 recession.

The robust growth environment and tightening labor market conditions resulted in a self-supporting loop of rising prices and wages. This wage-price feedback loop and the expanding deficit prompted President Johnson to advance a tax hike as a means of controlling inflation. The Revenue and Expenditure Control Act of 1968 was passed on June

Consumer Price Index 1968–1969,
Semi-annual and Annual Percent

Six-month Periods:	Annualized Percentage Change
December 1967 to June 1968	4.6
June 1968 to December 1968	4.7
December 1968 to June 1969	6.4
June 1969 to December 1969	5.9
Twelve-month Periods:	
December 1967 to December 1968	4.7
December 1968 to December 1969	6.1

Source: Recession Prevention Handbook, Norman Frumkin, 2010

28, but the tax hikes were made retroactive to January 1 for corporations, and April 1 for households. The act imposed a 10 percent surcharge on individual and corporate taxes. Low-income families were completely exempt from the surcharge. In 1969, Congress renewed the surcharge through the middle of 1970 but reduced it to 5 percent. Besides higher taxes, monetary policy was also used to rein in the economy as the expansion extended and pushed inflation higher. Specifically, headline consumer prices accelerated to a 6.4 percent annualized rate during the first six months of 1969 after recording a 4.7 percent advance in 1968.

The makers of domestic monetary policy were generally supportive of the robust growth environment during the first few years of the expansion, as the Federal Open Market Committee (FOMC) saw its role as supporting growth and achieving full employment. As a result, the federal funds rate was held between 3 percent and 4 percent during the trough of the 1961–1964 period in which growth averaged 4.5 percent per year. Supportive monetary policy remained in place even as growth of 5.5 percent was recorded in 1965. Short-term rates were temporarily pushed above 6 percent in 1966 and early 1967, but as growth slowed, the Federal Reserve again cut rates back to 4 percent in 1967. By the end of that year, it was clear that wages and prices were rising sharply, and the Fed was forced to begin a series of rate hikes that peaked at 10.5 percent in mid-1969. Longer-term rates began to climb steadily from a 4.3 percent low in March 1966 to a peak of 8.43 percent in the first week of January 1970. The rate hikes begun in 1968, combined with that year's fiscal tightening, set the stage for the downturn.

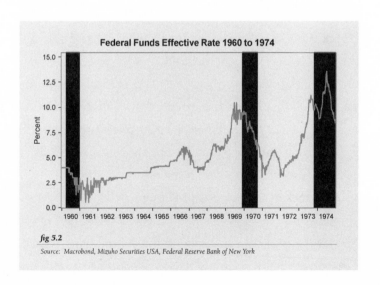

fig 5.2

Source: *Macrobond, Mizuho Securities USA, Federal Reserve Bank of New York*

A combination of higher taxes, the unwind of the US involvement in the Vietnam War, and rate hikes orchestrated by the Federal Reserve were complemented by a two-month United Auto Workers (UAW) union strike against General Motors in 1970. At the time, the effect of four hundred thousand highly paid auto workers walking off the job was estimated to have added 0.4 percent to the civilian jobless rate, and cut real GNP by upward of 1.1 percent. The political pressure that management had to bear, due to the strike's impact on the economy, resulted in a contraction that pushed the economy into another downturn sixteen months later, in November 1973. The 1970 UAW contract restored the cost of living adjustment to approximately 0.5 percent of total non-farm employment and increased already lavish healthcare benefits to UAW workers at GM. The fact that the strike was so well anticipated is seen as a cause for the downturn, as parts were stockpiled and then run down during the work stoppage.

Changes in Auto and Other Gross National Product During 1970
[Billions of Dollars, Seasonally Adjusted Annual Rates]

Period GNP		Change from Preceding Quarter		
		Auto GNP	All Other GNP	
1970:	I	7.8	-4.7	12.5
	II	11.6	4.3	7.3
	III	14.4	-0.7	15.1
	IV	5.4	-12.0	17.4

Source: Department of Commerce, Economic Report of the President, 1971

The largest bankruptcy in history also helped bring an end to the long postwar expansion. Penn Central Transportation Company (Penn Central) was created in 1968 by the merger of New York Central and the New York, New Haven, and Hartford railroads. This mixed-use rail service had more than $5 billion in assets, 20,000 miles of tracks, and 180,000 employees, and was projected to generate $17 billion in operating revenue. However, the new company had only $13.3 million in cash, and this amalgam of struggling companies was doomed from the outset. Competition from trucks and the expanding highway system resulted in a $150 million loss in its first year of operation, and the next two years were even worse, leaving banks unwilling to loan Penn Central additional funds and forcing it to file for bankruptcy protection in June 1970.

Real growth declined by 0.9 percent in the fourth quarter of 1969, followed by a 2.9 percent decline in the first quarter of 1970. Growth temporarily picked up during the middle two quarters of the year, followed by a 3.3 percent decline in the final quarter of 1970. The recession was cut short because the Federal Reserve began reducing rates sharply in February 1970, pushing them down by 6.5 percent to just 3 percent in the final days of 1970. After reaching a peak at 8.43 percent the week of January 2, 1969, rates stayed high until that August, before declining to 5.5 percent in December. Fiscal policy also did its share in reversing the downturn—the $9 billion fiscal surplus recorded in 1969 turned into an $11 billion deficit in 1970 as built-in income support programs kicked in.

Federal Government Receipts and Expenditures, National Income Accounts Basis, 1969–70
[Billions of Dollars, Seasonally Adjusted Annual Rates]

Period	Actual			Full Employment Estimates		
	Receipts	Expenditures	Surplus or Deficit (-)	Receipts	Expenditures	Surplus
1969	200.6	191.3	9.3	203.3	191.7	11.7
1970	195.4	206.2	-10.8	212.0	205.3	6.7
1969: I	197.2	187.7	9.5	197.2	188.1	9.1
II	202.5	189.1	13.4	203.4	189.5	13.9
III	200.8	192.5	8.3	204.3	192.8	11.5
IV	202.0	195.9	6.1	208.3	196.2	12.1
1970: I	195.9	197.7	-1.7	208.0	197.6	10.4
II	196.7	210.9	-14.2	211.9	209.9	2.0
III	194.9	206.7	-11.8	211.9	205.5	6.4
IV	194.1	209.5	-15.4	216.2	208.3	7.9

Source: Department of Commerce and Council of Economic Advisers, Economic Report of the President, 1971

Chapter 6

The 1973–1975 Oil Crisis Recession

The sixth recession of the postwar period lasted sixteen months and was the longest and deepest—and in many ways, the most important contraction—in the economy until the financial crisis recession of December 2007. A number of key developments that reshaped the global economic and geopolitical landscape preceded the downturn, including the Nixon wage and price controls, the collapse of Bretton Woods, and the first Arab oil embargo—all of which occurred during a bear market in stocks, and a rapid unwind from the Vietnam War. The emergence of newly industrialized countries also increased competition in a number of key industries that were the core drivers of the domestic economy in the period immediately following World War II. The Nixon resignation also occurred during this period, but the first key development of the period would be the emergence of stagflation in the UK and then in the US.

Not only did the economy experience stubbornly high inflation before and after the recession, but the jobless rate did not peak until May 1975, even though the recession ended in March. The confluence of events resulted in a combination of fiscal and monetary policy tightening. As the war in Southeast Asia was unwinding, government defense spending reduced sharply, as did the ranks of active-duty military personnel. Rising long-term rates and Fed rate hikes also helped cause the downturn as household spending on durable goods contracted. A government pullback in housing subsidies also played a part in the recession as housing starts slowed sharply. The result was a broad, deep, and long downturn that would span both the Nixon and Ford administrations. It would remain a factor in the U-shaped recovery that confronted the Carter team in the White House, and it would still be a factor in the early days of the Reagan presidency.

The November 1973 to March 1975 recession would witness the development of a wage and price spiral, and the advent of stagflation. These two developments would set the stage for a shift in focus from post-Depression Keynesianism to Milton Friedman's monetarism and start the second phase of the postwar period that would last until the early 1990s.

The economy heading into the 1973–1975 recession was different in nature from that which had been experienced during the prior six contractions. Stagflation got its name during this recession—it is defined as a stagnant economic environment during a period of high underemployment and high inflation. Postwar Keynesianism was centered on the predicted trade-off between unemployment and inflation depicted by the Phillips curve. This relationship suggested that policymakers could run the economy a little hot to pull down the jobless rate, so long as they were willing to allow inflation to pick up. In the early 1970s, this relationship began to break down, and economists were hard-pressed to explain its failure. During the 1973–1975 recession, there were five quarters when the economy contracted, yet the unemployment rate peaked at 9 percent two months after the trough had been passed, in March 1975. Inflation tripled in 1973, rising to 9.6 percent from 3.4 percent, and it remained between 10 percent and 12 percent from February 1974 to April 1975.

Stagflation in the 1970s

Quarterly Annualized Growth	Q1	Q2	Q3	Q4
1973	1.2%	4.6%	-2.2%	3.8%
1974	-3.3%	1.1%	-3.8%	-1.6%
1975	-4.7%	3.1%	6.8%	5.5%

Source: The Balance, July 2, 2017

The roots of stagflation were spread far and wide within the economy by the late 1960s. President Nixon had inherited a recession from Lyndon B. Johnson, who had simultaneously launched his Great Society initiative and greatly expanded the Vietnam War. Despite public sentiment against the war, Congress reluctantly continued to fund it, as Nixon searched for a diplomatic solution. By the time Nixon was up for reelection, Congress agreed to a large expansion in Social Security, and Nixon won his second term. The inflation of the early 1970s was also blamed on: 1) a fourfold rise in oil prices; 2) currency speculators driving down the dollar; 3) greedy businessmen and even greedier unions; and 4) a monetary policy that financed the growing budget deficits.

The expansion that preceded the 1973–1975 recession lasted just thirty-six months, from November 1970 to November 1973, making it the shortest expansion in the postwar period to date. Despite its short duration, the expansion was characterized by solid economic growth. Real GNP expanded by 4.8 percent in the first quarter of 1972 and accelerated to an exceptionally strong 9.5 percent in the second quarter of the year. This spike in real GNP was followed by increases ranging from 5.8 percent to 8.6 percent in the next three quarters. This strong growth environment resulted in a steady rise in capacity utilization, from 77.9 percent in 1971 to 87.6 percent in 1973. As the utilization rate increased, the jobless rate declined. In early 1972, the civilian jobless rate stood at 5.9 percent and fell steadily to 4.5 percent by October 1973, approaching the 4 percent estimated level. As a result of this growth environment and the resulting increase in utilization of existing factories and equipment, as well as the decline in the pool of available workers, inflation surged from 3.4 percent to 8.8 percent between December 1971 and December 1972.

The 1973 acceleration in inflation would be reflected in workers' earnings, setting the stage for a wage-price spiral and stagflation. Although demand for workers was strong in 1973, and several union contracts were up for renewal that year, there were no strikes. Earnings were bolstered by an increasing

Jobless Rate, 1972–1973

	1972	1973
Jan	5.9	5.0
Feb	5.8	5.1
Mar	5.9	5.0
April	5.8	5.0
May	5.8	5.0
June	5.5	4.8
July	5.6	4.7
Aug	5.6	4.8
Sept	5.5	4.8
Oct	5.5	4.5
Nov	5.2	4.7
Dec	5.1	4.9

Source: Recession Prevention Handbook, Norman Frumkin, 2010

number of workers who were covered by cost-of-living adjustments (COLAs) that compensated them for the loss of purchasing power, due to inflation. The number of workers covered by COLAs increased to more than four million in 1973, from two million in the mid-1960s. By linking wages to prices, corporate margins were being squeezed by rising commodity costs.

Crude oil prices surged by more than 40 percent between October 19, 1973, and March 1974 as the per-barrel price rose from $2.90 to $11.65. Other raw material prices rose by upward of 10 percent during this period, leading to a secondary rise in prices.

The wage-price spiral prompted the Fed to sharply hike short-term interest rates, and prompted a 40 percent decline in the Dow Jones Industrial Average (DJIA) over a 694-day bear market in stocks between January 11, 1973, and December 6, 1974. Long-term rates also rose and, when combined with reduced government subsidies for housing, tipped the economy over the end. The federal funds rate rose from 3.4 percent in January 1972 to 5.3 percent in December, and subsequently peaked at 10.8 percent in September 1973. The yield on the 10-year Treasury note also rose during this period to a cycle high of 7.5 percent in August 1973, from a low of 6.3 percent in November 1972, resulting in a yield curve inversion. This led to a disintermediation in the banking industry, causing bank lending to shrink and the economy to contract.

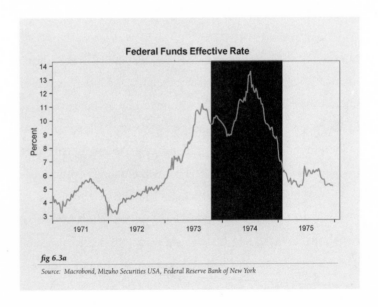

fig 6.3a

Source: *Macrobond, Mizuho Securities USA, Federal Reserve Bank of New York*

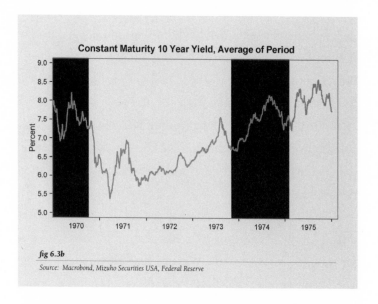

Constant Maturity 10 Year Yield, Average of Period

fig 6.3b

Source: *Macrobond, Mizuho Securities USA, Federal Reserve*

The great inflation of the early 1970s came about from a confluence of factors outside the expansion of union contracts covered by COLAs. Inflation pressures were evident early in the expansion as the dollar came under siege in the currency markets. The Nixon administration's decision in 1971 to end gold convertibility, and introduce wage-price controls, inadvertently amplified the problem, while the Arab oil embargo of 1973–1974 was the final and most disruptive contributor to the recession.

The White House undertook a series of economic measures—the "Nixon Shock"—to address inflation and its adverse effect on the Bretton Woods currency system that was established after World War II, to maintain stable exchange rates and stimulate the rebuilding effort. On August 15, 1971, President Nixon unilaterally ended the convertibility of US dollars into gold. Although he did not technically abolish the Bretton Woods system, it had clearly outlived its usefulness. For example, as early as 1966, non-US central banks held $414 billion in US dollars, while the Treasury had only $13.2 billion in gold reserves, of which only $3.2 billion were available to cover foreign holdings of the US currency. At that time, the US unemployment rate was 6.1 percent and the inflation rate was 5.8 percent.

The increase in inflation was viewed as a direct consequence of the US abusing its privilege to print money to pay for its unpopular Vietnam War and the growing cost of its social contract that had been expanded by Lyndon B. Johnson. By 1971, the Fed's M2 money supply measure increased by 10 percent, and by May, West Germany left the postwar currency system, unwilling to devalue its own currency and risk importing US inflation. As a result, other nations within the Bretton Woods system began to redeem their dollars for gold, and the Treasury needed to stem the tide of redemptions. Then, on August 5, 1971, Congress released its report recommending a devaluation of the dollar to protect the currency. Four days later, Switzerland left the exchange rate system and the dollar dropped against all European currencies in the open market. This prompted the Nixon team into action.

On August 15, to address the core inflationary consequences of the currency devaluation, a policy shift imposed a ninety-day freeze on wages and prices, and a temporary 10 percent surcharge on imports, that was to be lifted by year's end. The freeze on wages and prices was the first comprehensive implementation of this emergency tool since the end of World War II, while the import surcharge was designed to make US products more competitive. The short-term success of these initiatives would eventually be overshadowed by their longer-term consequences. In particular, the decision not to lift controls on oil and gasoline would create an artificial shortage that was exacerbated by the 1973–1974 oil embargo. The result was the rationing of gasoline at the consumer level, and the long lines that followed at service stations around the country which had a major psychological effect on the country, for years.

The ninety-day freeze on wages and prices was successful in the short-term, as was phase 2 of the controls, requiring wage and price increases to stay within strict guidelines overseen by the Cost of Living Board. However, in 1973, the phase 3 controls, which relaxed allowable price and wage increase standards, and weakened their enforcement, failed miserably and resulted in a spike in inflation. The Federal Reserve responded by continuing the tightening of credit that had begun in 1972. This tightening constrained the economy and triggered the recession.

The 1973–1974 oil embargo also played a critical role in the behavior of policymakers in this cycle. Not only was the oil embargo an immediate inflation development, but more important, it biased up underlying longer-term inflation. Union COLAs embedded higher prices in wages while higher energy prices rendered a significant share of the existing capital stock effectively obsolete, overnight.

The oil embargo was triggered by President Nixon's

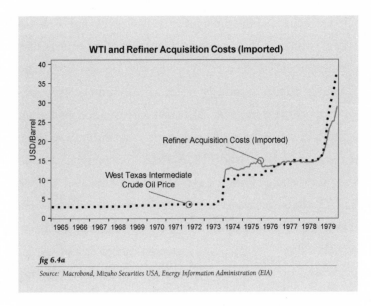

fig 6.4a

Source: Macrobond, Mizuho Securities USA, Energy Information Administration (EIA)

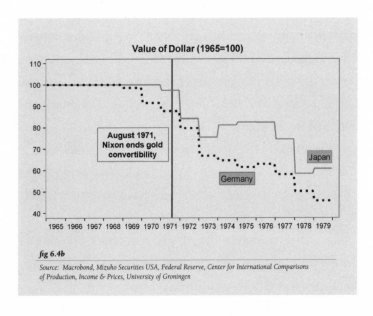

fig 6.4b

Source: Macrobond, Mizuho Securities USA, Federal Reserve, Center for International Comparisons of Production, Income & Prices, University of Groningen

October 19 request to Congress to make available $2.2 billion in emergency aid to Israel for the Yom Kippur War. The emergency funding for Israel was the political excuse for the Organization of Petroleum Exporting Countries (OPEC) to increase the price of imported crude oil and initiate a series of production cuts that would alter the world price of oil. These cuts nearly quadrupled the price of oil, from $2.90 a barrel to $11.65 a barrel, by January 1974.

The actual reason behind the embargo had to do with the fixed-dollar price of oil, which squeezed producers' purchasing power as US inflation rose and the dollar declined, following the breakdown of the Bretton Woods currency agreement. This, and the fact that non-OPEC petroleum exporters' share of the world crude oil market was declining, gave Arab producers increased market power to protect their purchasing power from the rising price of all dollar-based commodity prices that were up around 10 percent by that year alone. By March 1974, OPEC members were disagreeing over the long-term benefits of their new pricing policy and whether it would be sustainable. Cheating by members to increase market share led OPEC to officially lift the embargo in 1974, but the price had already started to decline in the wake of increased supply.

Consumer inflation psychology had also been altered. It resulted in long-term detrimental effects on the economy and a generally higher interest rate environment. Policymakers looked to curtail demand amid reduced supply, which led to a combination of demand-pull and cost-push inflation for the first time since the end of World War II. The financial markets reacted to these new macro fundamentals, not only in the oil market, but also in the bond and money markets by entering a long-term bear market. Between January 11, 1973, and December 6, 1974 (694 days), the DJIA lost more than 45 percent of its market value, making it one of the worst bear markets in the long history of the index. This added to the growing pessimism and the feeling of falling behind that helped trigger the recession.

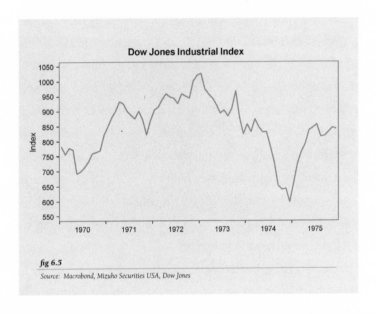

fig 6.5

Source: Macrobond, Mizuho Securities USA, Dow Jones

Chapter 7

The January to July 1980
Carter Credit Control Recession

The first recession of the 1980s lasted only six months, and was preceded by an average fifty-eight-month expansion. This recession, however, was followed by a twelve-month expansion, resulting in the first back-to-back (double-dip) recession of the postwar period. In fact, since the 1980 recession was so quickly followed by the July 1981–November 1982 downturn, some economists lump them into one recessionary cycle. This analysis leaves them separated because, even though inflation had a lot to do with both contractions, the imposition of credit controls was a key contributor to the first contraction, while an inverted yield curve dominated the second.

The back-to-back recessions resulted from a sharp acceleration in inflation in the 1970s that led to stagflation. This period of high inflation and high unemployment called for aggressive policy action. In 1980, President Carter invoked the Credit Control Act of 1969, in response to inflation, which had climbed to an 18 percent annual rate that March. The Federal Reserve was instructed to limit credit card extensions and other unsecured consumer loans. The result was a 9.1 percent plunge in second quarter real GDP after a 1.5 percent first quarter decline. The powerful psychological and real effect of the controls caused President Carter to begin phasing them out in May and lifting them in July; the economy rebounded quickly. Congress, angered by the resulting spike in joblessness to 7.5 percent by May 1980, from 6 percent, voted to rescind the president's authority to implement credit controls again in July 1982.

The credit controls were preceded by an aggressive Fed tightening initiated by Paul Volcker, who was appointed Fed chairman in a cabinet shakeup by the Carter team, in August 1979. This shakeup moved previous Fed Chairman G. William Miller to the position of Treasury secretary.

The first Volcker tightening began in late 1979 and pushed the Fed's discount rate from 10 percent to 12 percent in just two months, and the prime rate climbed to an unprecedented 20 percent by March 1980. The collapse in real GDP in the second quarter led not only to the lifting of the credit controls, but also to a decline in inflation and a drop in interest rates that helped lift the economy out of this short, but sharp slump.

The economic downturn that began in January 1980 and ended abruptly that July was unique. Not only because the recession proved to be the first of two, separated by only one year of growth, but it was also the most anticipated contraction of the postwar period. The Council of Economic Advisers had projected a "mild and brief" downturn in the *Economic Report of the President* transmitted to Congress that January. If taken in totality, however, the 1980 and 1981 recessions would be the most severe contraction in the first thirty-five years of the postwar period. In the first two quarters of 1980, the economy contracted by 2.3 percent and 9.1 percent, respectively. This sharp drop in activity explains why the Carter team quickly reversed gears after imposing credit controls on the economy, and why Congress later removed the president's ability to constrict bank lending.

The seeds of the 1980 and 1981 contractions were sown in the inflationary cycle that emerged in the mid- to late-1970s, as a confluence of factors pushed inflation into double-digit territory. Three factors are generally credited with dominating the 1978–1979 economic environment that led to the Carter credit controls, and the Fed's shift from interest rates to money supply targeting:

1. A marked slowdown in productivity accelerated in the 1970s.

2. The Iranian Revolution of 1979 resulted in higher gasoline and other crude oil product prices.

3. Import prices surged as the exchange value of the dollar plunged.

These developments not only exacerbated the problem with accelerating inflation that had been building for years, but also hampered attempts to stimulate economic growth and boost employment. Policymakers found themselves at a loss to deal with accelerating inflation even though the economy had failed to come close to full employment since the end of the 1973–1975 recession.

The economic expansion that followed the 1973–1975 recession was not particularly robust, and unemployment remained relatively high through the full fifty-three months of its term. Specifically, joblessness had declined to only 5.9 percent in both August and September 1978 from a high rate of 6.1 percent in July 1975. It subsequently fluctuated around 5.7 percent between October 1978 and July 1979. The unemployment rate then increased as the expansion extended, ranging between 5.5 percent and 6.2 percent in the month prior to the 1980 downturn in the economy. As the recession took hold, the jobless rate increased further to 7 percent in April, and then 7.7 percent in May, before climbing to 7.8 percent that June. Moreover, the slack evident in the economy as the 1975–1979 expansion matured was also apparent in a higher jobless rate for experienced workers. This suggests that it was not just a baby boom–induced problem. In fact, the jobless rate for experienced workers in 1978–1979 was a full half percent to 1.5 percent above that which prevailed in comparable periods, prior to the onset of the three previous recessions.

The slack in the labor market was not reflected in the rate of capacity utilization. In fact, capacity utilization rose to 84.2 percent in 1979, from 82.4 percent in 1977, indicating that the economy was approaching full utilization of manufacturing capacity. But this increase in utilization never pushed the economy to the point that companies were forced to bring older and less efficient equipment back online, a development that could account for the rise in inflation. This unique situation seems to reflect the fact that industrial production was slowing into the final year of the expansion.

A marked slowing in the housing market was also evident in the economy as the expansion moved into its final stages. Starts of new homes fell by 275.2 thousand units in 1979, and as a result, household spending on durable goods like furniture, appliances, and autos also declined. Despite the expansion being lackluster, and the slack evident in the labor market, inflation continued to rise. According to statistical data published at the time, the consumer price index (CPI) accelerated to a 16 percent annualized increase between December 1979 and June 1980, from a 7.9 percent annualized rate experienced between June and December 1978.

Consumer Price Index in Real Time

Six-Month Periods	Annualized Percentage Change
June 1978 to December 1978	7.9
December 1978 to June 1979	14.7
June 1979 to December 1979	12.7
December 1979 to June 1980	16.0

Source: Bureau of Labor Statistics, U.S. Department of Labor

This acceleration in inflation has been the subject of much debate, but it is fairly clear that a decline in productivity, the Iranian Revolution, and a declining exchange value of the dollar were key contributors. However, a spike in food prices was also an important consideration, as was the spike in mortgage interest rates:

- The slowing in productivity growth experienced during the 1970s prevented this important macro consideration from increasing labor costs. In the 1970s, wage and benefit costs increased as Social Security payroll taxes and unemployment insurance payments made by employers increased, and, combined with higher federally mandated minimum wages, pushed up labor costs. Without offsetting productivity gains, businesses were forced to increase prices to maintain margins.

- The Iranian Revolution in 1979 was another important inflationary development. Although global oil supply decreased by only 4 percent as a result of the crisis in Iran, widespread panic over supply disruptions caused crude oil prices to more than double to $39.5 per barrel over a twelve-month period. This increase flowed quickly through to the cost of other energy products, especially gasoline prices, as long lines appeared at service stations for a second time in the decade. The increased costs filtered through to the price of every product, as energy input costs rose, and companies strived to again maintain margins.

- A 10 percent decline in the dollar in the late 1970s contributed to higher import prices, allowing domestic manufacturers to pass on increased costs without any competition from overseas producers.

- Food prices surged in 1977–1978, as falling beef production was complemented by rising prices for pork and poultry due to severe winter weather in both years, increased disease, rising feed costs, and increased government regulation. During the eight quarters of the 1978–1979 period, food prices increased at a 10.3 percent annual rate, while the volatility of food prices rose to a high 4.9 percent, leading to increased uncertainty.

- The acceleration in inflation led to higher interest rates, which also filtered through to the monthly CPI data, in the form of higher mortgage interest. The mortgage rate contribution to the CPI, in fact, accelerated from just 0.2 percent in 1977 to 3.7 percent in 1980.

Rates of Increase of Food Prices, 1977–80 and 1972–75

	1977	1978	1979	1980
1st quarter	6.1	10.9	15.2	3.6
2d quarter	6.0	17.3	6.2	5.8
3d quarter	4.5	9.6	4.9	16.7
4th quarter	5.6	9.9	10.1	16.0
	1972	1973	1974	1975
1st quarter	6.7	14.0	16.8	5.0
2d quarter	2.5	17.8	7.4	3.0
3d quarter	5.4	18.3	5.9	12.2
4th quarter	6.5	15.1	13.5	5.0

Source: Bureau of Economic Analysis

Alternative Annual Inflation Rates, 1977–80

Period	All-Items CPI	CPI Excluding Mortgage Interest	Contribution
Dec. 1976–Dec. 1977	6.8	6.6	0.2
Dec. 1977–Dec. 1978	9.0	8.2	0.8
Dec. 1978–Dec. 1979	13.3	11.6	1.7
Dec. 1979–Jun. 1980	14.8	11.1	3.7
Jun. 1980–Dec. 1980	9.9	10.9	-1.0

Source: BLS

Policymakers' response to this acceleration in inflation, despite evidence of slack labor market conditions, resulted in the 1980 recession. The first major policy shift was undertaken by the Federal Reserve in the wake of the acceleration in inflation, and the loss of confidence in the exchange value of the dollar. On October 6, 1979, the Volcker Fed announced three major changes in monetary policy, designed to make policy more restrictive, in an effort to rein in inflation. First, the Fed announced an increase in the discount rate to 12 percent. Second, marginal reserve requirements were increased to 8 percent against deposit liabilities. And third, the Fed shifted its day-to-day open market operations from targeting short-term rates to targeting money supply. These changes resulted in a sharp increase in short-term interest rates and an increase in interest rate volatility. The federal funds rate increased to a peak of 19.85 percent in early April 1980, from about 10 percent in June 1979. The yield on the 10-year Treasury note rose four hundred basis points between June 1979 and its peak of 13 percent in February 1980.

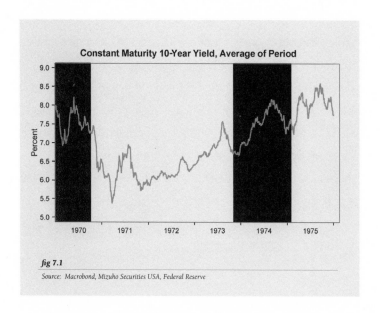

fig 7.1

Source: *Macrobond, Mizuho Securities USA, Federal Reserve*

With inflation continuing to accelerate into 1980 despite the Fed's actions, the Carter team instructed the Fed to impose a series of restraints on credit to help rein in inflation in March of that year. Banks were asked to limit loan growth to between 6 percent and 9 percent in 1980. Consumer creditors and credit card issuers were required to deposit 15 percent of their increase in certain consumer loans into non–interest bearing accounts at the Federal Reserve. Many key lending categories such as auto loans, mortgages, and home improvement loans were exempt. Additionally, a 3 percent surcharge was added to the discount rate paid by large banks that repeatedly borrowed from the discount window. The reserve requirement on managed liabilities (deposits that banks solicit from other banks) was increased from 8 percent to 10 percent. Restraints were also imposed on the amount of credit raised by nonmember banks, and curbs were put on the expansion of assets acquired by money market mutual funds. These credit restraints proved to be a blunt policy tool and crippled the expansion, causing a 9.1 percent plunge in the economy during the second quarter of 1980. The speed with which these credit controls slowed the economy was fully unexpected, and as a result, they were phased out as soon as it became clear how effective they were at choking off growth.

Chapter 8

1981–1982 Iranian Energy Crisis Recession

After only twelve months of expansion, between July 1980 and July 1981, the economy slipped back into a recession, and this time, the contraction was the deepest experienced in the postwar period. This is the first and only back-to-back recession on record, according to the National Bureau of Economic Research. The first leg of the double-dip recession has been credited principally to the Carter credit controls, while the second downturn is often referred to as the Reagan Recession. In reality, it should be credited to the aggressive tightening in monetary policy orchestrated by then–Fed Chairman Paul Volcker, who took the battle against inflation to an unprecedented level. The result was a broad-based, brutal recession with virtually every part of the economy sharing the economic pain inflicted by the Fed's desire to break the back of the wage-price spiral, and end stagflation.

Mining, construction, and manufacturing were the worst-hit areas, scoring 90 percent of all job losses. The jobless rate is another indicator of the depth of the downturn, and although the jobless rate stayed high after the July 1980 trough (7.8 percent), it peaked at 10.8 percent in December 1982. The 10.8 percent unemployment rate was the highest recorded since the Great Depression. Several regions experienced joblessness well above the national average. Michigan led the nation in September 1982 with an unemployment rate of 14.5 percent, while Alabama was close behind at 14.3 percent. West Virginia was third, with an unemployment rate of 14.1 percent. The Youngstown-Warren, Ohio/Pennsylvania Metropolitan area had a jobless rate of 18.7 percent—the highest of all metro areas—in contrast to the 3.5 percent jobless rate recorded in Stamford, Connecticut.

Inflation, which had averaged 3.2 percent in the postwar period, more than doubled to 7.7 percent after the 1972 oil shock, and continued to climb to 9.1 percent by 1975. The long 1973–1975 recession caused inflation to dip to 5.8 percent in 1976 before climbing to 11.3 percent in 1979 and 13.5 percent in 1980. Double-digit inflation reduced the value of the dollar, and prompted the Volcker Fed to shift from interest rates to money supply targeting. The result was a spike in short rates, which pushed the funds rate up to 20 percent by June 1981, while the prime rate peaked at 21.5 percent a year later. The result was consolidation that affected most categories included in real GDP, especially consumer spending on durable goods, residential and nonresidential investment spending, exports, as well as all four categories of government spending.

The recession began in July 1981 and ended in November 1982. It would prove to be the deepest contraction in the thirty-five years since World War II ended in September 1945. This was also the only recession preceded by an exceptionally short twelve-month expansion. The pending contraction in economic activity was quickly recognized by the Reagan administration, which had replaced the Carter team in January 1981. President Reagan used the projected double dip as leverage to get his supply-side tax cut enacted that summer. The Kemp-Roth tax cut, or the Economic Recovery Tax Act of 1981 (ERTA), has been cited as one of the key factors that pushed interest rates up to unprecedented levels during the recession, especially in 1982, exacerbating the consolidation in the economy. The tax cut pushed the budget deficit to unprecedented levels in both absolute and relative terms, resulting in increased competition for loanable funds between the public and private sectors. This crowding out served to increase rates as the Fed contracted liquidity in an attempt to wring inflation out of an economy that had become embedded in a wage-price spiral.

From 1960 to 1970, the headline consumer price index had increased to an average rate of 2.2 percent per year. Between 1970 and 1973, the average rate of inflation by this key measure accelerated to 4.9 percent. Then, aggravated by the sharp jump in world energy prices and an unexpected decline in productivity, inflation climbed to 11.1 percent in 1974, but by 1976, it had slowed to 5.8 percent. In the next few years, which included a second oil price shock, caused by the Iranian Revolution, inflation climbed each year to a peak of 13.5 percent in 1980. The recession slowed inflation to 10.4 percent, but average hourly earnings accelerated in 1981 from 6.9 percent to 8.5 percent, leading to concerns that inflation expectations had become entrenched in wage negotiations. This link between prices and wages was reflected in the increased use of cost-of-living adjustments in union contracts and non-union wage decisions. In fact, hourly compensation data for the nonfarm business sector show that double-digit wage gains were broad-based in 1980 and 1981, with overall hourly compensation rising by 10.8 percent in 1980. Hourly earnings in the heavily unionized manufacturing industries, on the other hand, were up 12.7 percent. In 1981, hourly earnings were up 9 percent and 8 percent, respectively.

Changes in Consumer Price Indexes, Commodities, and Services, 1948–82 [Percent Change]

Year	All Items		Commodities						Services		Energy (2)	
			Total		Food		Commodities Less Food					
	Dec. to Dec. (1)	Year to Year	Dec. to Dec. (1)	Year to Year	Dec. to Dec. (1)	Year to year	Dec. to Dec. (1)	Year to Year	Dec. to Dec. (1)	Year to Year	Dec. to Dec. (1)	Year to Year
1948	2.7	7.8	1.7	7.2	-0.8	8.5	5.3	7.7	6.1	6.3	N/A	N/A
1949	-1.8	-1.0	-4.1	-2.6	-3.7	-4.0	-4.8	-1.5	3.6	4.8	N/A	N/A
1950	5.8	1.0	7.7	0.6	9.6	1.4	5.7	-0.1	3.6	3.2	N/A	N/A
1951	5.9	7.9	5.9	9.0	7.4	11.1	4.6	7.5	5.2	5.3	N/A	N/A
1952	0.9	2.2	-0.7	1.3	-1.1	1.8	-0.5	0.9	4.6	4.4	N/A	N/A
1953	0.6	0.8	-0.6	-0.3	-1.3	-1.5	0.2	0.2	4.2	4.3	N/A	N/A
1954	-0.5	0.5	-1.4	-0.9	-1.6	-0.2	-1.4	-1.1	1.9	3.3	N/A	N/A

1955	0.4	-0.4	-0.4	-0.9	-0.9	-1.4	0	-0.7	2.3	2.0	N/A	N/A
1956	2.9	1.5	2.6	0.9	3.1	0.7	2.5	1.0	3.1	2.5	N/A	N/A
1957	3.0	3.6	2.6	3.1	2.8	3.3	2.2	3.1	4.5	4.0	N/A	N/A
1958	1.8	2.7	1.3	2.3	2.2	4.2	0.8	1.1	2.7	3.8	-0.7	0.2
1959	1.5	0.8	0.6	0.1	-0.8	-1.6	1.5	1.3	3.7	2.9	4.3	1.7
1960	1.5	1.6	1.1	0.9	3.1	1.0	-0.3	0.4	2.7	3.3	1.5	2.6
1961	0.7	1.0	0	0.5	-0.9	1.3	0.6	0.3	1.9	2.0	-1.1	0.2
1962	1.2	1.1	1.0	0.9	1.5	0.9	0.7	0.7	1.7	1.9	2.1	0.3
1963	1.6	1.2	1.4	0.9	1.9	1.4	1.2	0.7	2.3	2.0	-0.8	0.3
1964	1.2	1.3	0.8	1.1	1.4	1.3	0.4	0.8	1.8	1.9	-0.2	-0.4
1965	1.9	1.7	1.6	1.2	3.4	2.2	0.7	0.6	2.6	2.2	2.0	1.8
1966	3.4	2.9	2.5	2.6	3.9	5.0	1.9	1.4	4.9	3.9	1.8	1.6
1967	3.0	2.9	2.5	1.8	1.2	0.9	3.1	2.6	4.0	4.4	1.4	2.2
1968	4.7	4.2	3.8	3.7	4.3	3.6	3.7	3.7	6.1	5.2	1.7	1.5
1969	6.1	5.4	5.5	4.5	7.2	5.1	4.5	4.2	7.4	6.9	3.1	2.7
1970	5.5	5.9	4.0	4.7	2.2	5.5	4.8	4.1	8.2	8.1	4.5	2.7
1971	3.4	4.3	2.9	3.4	4.3	3.0	2.3	3.8	4.1	5.6	3.1	3.9
1972	3.4	3.3	3.4	3.0	4.7	4.3	2.5	2.2	3.6	3.8	2.8	2.8
1973	8.8	6.2	10.4	7.4	20.1	14.5	5.0	3.4	6.2	4.4	16.8	8.0
1974	12.2	11.0	12.7	12.0	12.2	14.4	13.2	10.6	11.3	9.3	21.6	29.3
1975	7.0	9.1	6.3	8.9	6.5	8.5	6.2	9.2	8.1	9.5	11.6	10.6
1976	4.8	5.8	3.3	4.3	0.6	3.1	5.1	5.0	7.3	8.3	6.9	7.2
1977	6.8	6.5	6.1	5.8	8.0	6.3	4.9	5.4	7.9	7.7	7.2	9.5
1978	9.0	7.7	8.9	7.1	11.8	10.0	7.7	5.8	9.3	8.5	8.0	6.3
1979	13.3	11.3	13.0	11.4	10.2	10.9	14.3	11.7	13.7	11.0	37.4	25.2

continued

1980	12.4	13.5	11.1	12.2	10.2	8.6	11.5	13.8	14.2	15.4	18.1	30.9
1981	8.9	10.4	6.0	8.4	4.3	7.9	6.7	8.6	13.0	13.1	11.9	13.5
1982	3.9	6.1	3.6	4.0	3.1	4.0	3.8	4.0	4.3	9.0	1.3	1.5

(1) Changes from December to December are based on unadjusted indexes
(2) Fuel oil, coal, and bottled gas; gas (piped) and electricity; and motor fuel, motor oil, coolant, etc.

Source: Economic Report of the President, 1983

Besides the acceleration in inflation that can be attributed to surging energy prices, and the link between wages and prices, a decline in nonfarm productivity was also evident in the late 1970s and early 1980s that attracted the attention of policymakers at the Fed and on Capitol Hill. Nonfarm productivity averaged 2.5 percent per year in the 1960s, but slowed to just 1.7 percent in the 1970s, and then to only 0.2 percent–0.3 percent in the first few years of the 1980s. This loss in productivity has been credited with the surge in the working age population as the baby boomers entered the labor force, as well as the increased obsolescence of energy-intensive capital goods in the new environment of high-cost energy. (See the energy price columns in Table 8.1). Between 1980 and 1981, the recession was also a factor in driving down productivity as output fell in four of the eight quarters (in two quarters of each year).

For the Volcker Fed, the slowing in productivity reflected a structural change in the economy, while the Reagan team saw it as a reflection of insufficient investment spending.

Essentially, the two designers of economic policy clashed over how to solve the problem of double-digit inflation and stagnant economic growth. The makers of domestic monetary policy pressured aggressive demand management, while the White House and Congress looked to ease inflation by expanding the supply side of the economy. The result was a deep recession marked by unprecedented joblessness, brought about by high interest rates, a surging currency, and a ballooning budget deficit.

The Fed's demand management policies resulted in sharply rising interest rates at the front end of the yield curve, while the rise in rates at the back end had been credited to rising inflation expectations and the clash between the public and private demands for credit. In an effort to break the back of rising inflation expectations, the Fed tightened reserve market conditions repeatedly between August 1980 and September 1981. The monthly average funds rate rose from 9.6 percent in August 1980 to 20.1 percent in January 1981, before declining to 14.9 percent that April. It then fluctuated between 18.3 percent and 18.9 percent between May and August, before falling to 16.9 percent in September, just before the second recession in three years started. This sharp rise in short-term interest rates increased bank-funding costs and slowed the pace of lending, heading into the recession.

Long-term interest rates also rose over this period, with the 10-year yield climbing from 12.57 percent in January 1981 to 15.32 percent that September. By early 1983, the 10-year yield had dropped to 10.46 percent. These higher long-term

Business Loans at Commercial Banks

	Quarterly Percentage Change at Annual Rate
1979	
I	21.0
II	18.1
III	19.5
IV	8.6
1980	
I	18.6
II	-10.7
III	14.3
IV	24.2
1981	
I	5.8
II	9.0

Source: Warren T. Trepeta, "Changes in Bank Lending Practices, 1979–81," Federal Reserve Bulletin, September 1981, Table 1, P. 671, Recession Prevention Handbook, Norman Frumkin, 2010

rates were reflected in mortgage rates, which rose from 12.5 percent in mid-1980 to 16 percent in May 1981. The result of higher rates along the yield curve was a 30 percent surge in the exchange value of the dollar, between August 1980 and a July 1981 peak. The currency resumed its upturn later in 1981, and finally peaked in early 1985 after another 55 percent advance. The increase in foreign competition was reflected in a 40 percent reduction in the net export surplus between 1980 and 1982, while the spike in interest rates chipped away at residential investment spending, and household spending on durable goods and equipment. Housing starts, in fact, plunged by 29.5 percent between December 1980 and June 1981, heading into the recession.

The demand management policies of the Fed were somewhat offset by the loose fiscal policy advanced by the Reagan White House. ERTA was designed to expand the supply side of the economy, and in the process, stimulate growth while restraining inflation. The resulting budget deficits pushed up the level of long-term rates, and drove up the dollar as higher rates attracted overseas investors.

The Reagan tax cut consisted of ten principal initiatives, each designed to increase supply by increasing incentives to simultaneously boost investment and savings in the economy. Workers were incentivized to increase their desire to work through a phased-in 23 percent cut in individual tax rates, over a three-year period. Individual tax brackets were also to be indexed to inflation beginning in 1985. The capital gains tax rate was cut from 28 percent to 20 percent, to encourage more long-term investments by households. The law also attempted to eliminate the marriage penalty by creating a 10 percent exclusion on income to two-earner couples, up to a maximum of $3,000. It increased the estate tax exemption to $600,000 from $175,625 and allowed all workers to establish individual retirement accounts (IRAs) while expanding employee stock ownership plans. The $200 interest exclusion was also replaced with a 15 percent net interest exclusion, capped at $900.

On the corporate side, the tax cut legislation created an accelerated cost recovery system to replace the traditional depreciation allowances, while also reducing the windfall profits tax. Although supporters and critics of this tax cut continue to debate its merits today, the change in the tax law did result in a ballooning of the budget deficit, both in absolute and relative terms. In its first year alone, the deficit grew by a factor of five times the prior year's receipt shortfall, and the deficit continued to deteriorate until 1986, when it hit a new peak in history to that date, at $221 billion.

Chapter 9

The July 1990–March 1991
Gulf War Recession

The eight-month 1990–1991 recession was preceded by the second longest expansion of the postwar period. The Reagan boom lasted nearly eight years (ninety-two months), but proved to be on shaky ground. As the November 1982 to July 1990 expansion progressed, signs of trouble began to surface.

On Monday, October 19, 1987, stock markets around the world crashed. Domestically, the Dow Jones Industrial Average (DJIA) lost more than 22 percent of its value. The crash was seen by many as evidence that investors were worried about accumulating inflation pressures associated with the record budget deficits that followed the Reagan tax cut. The savings and loan crisis also boiled over during the expansion, even though cracks in the thrift industry began to surface as far back as 1979. Forbearance simply exacerbated the problems, as did regulatory and tax reforms undertaken during the decade. The cost of cleaning up the savings and loan fiasco fell on taxpayers, and worsened an already bad budget deficit dynamic. Although the stock market crash and the savings and loan debacle were discrete events, they indicated the growing importance of financial markets in the economy. They also marked an important turning point in the postwar period, from inflation to credit cycles becoming the driving force behind the business cycle.

Other key developments that contributed to the 1990–1991 recession were the 1986 collapse in crude oil prices, cuts in defense spending as the Cold War came to an abrupt end with the fall of the Berlin Wall in 1989, and the contraction in economic activity following the launch of Operation Desert Storm that was dubbed the CNN effect. Demographic consideration also played a key role in the recession with a slowdown of new workers entering the labor market as Generation X replaced baby boomers. Two major natural disasters have also been credited with weakening the foundation of the Reagan expansion. Hurricane Hugo slammed into South Carolina in September 1989, and an earthquake near Loma Prieta rocked the San Francisco Bay area, a month later. The Federal Reserve also played a key role in upending the Reagan expansion, as did rising long-term interest rates.

The July 1990 to March 1991 recession proved to be relatively mild, by postwar standards, with real GDP declining for just two quarters—fourth quarter 1990 (minus 3.9 percent) and first quarter 1991 (minus 2.5 percent). Real GDP declined by only 0.1 percent in 1990, but rose by only 0.2 percent the following year, despite three quarters of rising GDP. The 1991 recovery was also unusually mild, and became known as the jobless recovery because the unemployment rate did not peak until nine months after the trough of the recession, at 7.1 percent in December 1991.

Some economists at the time suggested that the Reagan expansion simply ran out of steam and slipped into a shallow consolidation. Expansions, however, do not end on their own. Business cycles end because of external shocks to the economy, economic imbalances that build up during expansions, or inappropriate economic policies advanced by policymakers. All of these factors were at work in the 1990–1991 downturn, but the primary catalyst was the savings and loan crisis. This credit problem rippled through the economy in the late 1980s, and fundamentally weakened the economy's ability to deal with shocks. Most economists blame the invasion of Kuwait by Iraq and the sharp rise in energy prices from less than $19 per barrel in July 1990, to more than $30 per barrel in late August, and $40 per barrel in early October. Crude oil prices plunged immediately after Operation Desert Storm commenced and quickly liberated Kuwait. The live footage of the military campaign spearheaded by US forces from military bases quickly established inside Saudi Arabia captured the news headlines, and households were glued to their televisions to watch the conflict unfold on CNN and other news networks. Although it is natural to link an oil price shock with declines in business and consumer confidence, structural imbalances associated with the savings and loan crisis, exacerbated by the lagged effect of tightened monetary policy in 1988 and 1989, were the dominant drivers of the business cycle.

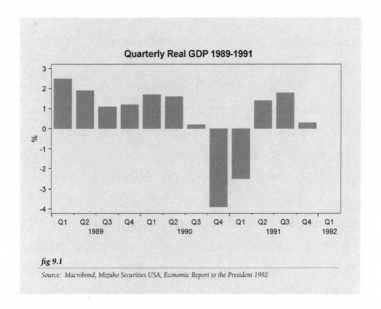

fig 9.1

Source: *Macrobond, Mizuho Securities USA, Economic Report to the President 1992*

The demise of the savings and loan industry began in 1979 when the Federal Reserve began its war on inflation, and inverted the yield curve through a series of rate hikes under its new money supply operating procedure. The thrift industry was built on issuing long-term mortgages at fixed rates, and financing them with short-term deposit liabilities. This quickly led to a liquidity squeeze, as savings and loans were limited as to how much they could pay on deposits. As the industry struggled, regulators moved to deregulate the industry, and exercised forbearance to keep this key source of liquidity to the housing market functioning. Two significant legislative initiatives, designed to aid the industry, resulted in huge, unintended consequences.

The Deposit Institution Deregulation and Monetary Control Act of 1980 and the Garn-St Germain Depository

Institutions Act of 1982 allowed thrifts to offer a wider array of savings products, including adjustable rate mortgages and commercial mortgages, that allowed them to make loans in states other than where they were chartered. Regulation Q interest rate ceilings were reduced, and so was regulatory oversight of the industry. The hope was that savings and loans would be able to grow their way out of the problems caused by their asset and liability mismatch. Instead, the industry's problems only got worse after the Reagan administration signed the Tax Reform Act of 1986, eliminating the ability of real estate investors to deduct passive losses against active income. This was a key tax shelter that had led to a boom in commercial construction in the early Reagan years, especially new apartment buildings. These projects were largely financed by the thrift industry, and when the tax shelter disappeared, property values plunged, burning through what little capital the savings and loan industry had left. The Federal Savings and Loan Insurance Corporation (FSLIC) resolved 296 institutions between 1986 and 1989, while the Resolution Trust Corporation (RTC) resolved 747 additional institutions between 1989 and 1995. The direct cost of the crisis has been placed at $160 billion, of which $132 billion came directly from taxpayers.

The bankruptcy of the FSLIC and the savings and loan crisis did not occur overnight; the disaster was waiting to happen for many years. It was exacerbated by policies designed to keep the industry going, even though it was clear that the fundamental problems confronting the industry were grave. In fact, fifteen public policies can be identified as having contributed to the crisis:

1. Savings and loans were charged the same federal deposit insurance premium, no matter how risky the institution's assets were.

2. Asset and liability mismatches were inherent in the structure of the industry, which did not foresee the inflation and interest rate developments of the 1960s–1970s.

3. Regulation Q limited the interest rate that institutions could pay on deposit liabilities.

4. A federal ban on adjustable rate mortgages magnified the problem for thrifts, forcing them into 30-year fixed-rate mortgages.

5. Restrictions on setting up branches and nationwide banking concentrated risk geographically.

6. Dual chartering, which permitted states to regulate savings and loans, allowed states to impose losses on federal taxpayers.

7. The secondary mortgage market created by the government under Fannie Mae and Freddie Mac undercut the profits of savings and loans.

8. The Fed's October 1979 shift to money supply from interest rate targeting led to an inverted yield curve.

9. Incomplete and bungled deregulation allowed S&Ls to make real estate loans without regard to geographic location, allowing them to hold up to 40 percent of their assets in commercial real estate loans.

10. Capital standards were debased in the early 1980s to keep the industry afloat. Generally accepted accounting standards were ignored, and goodwill rules were stretched to allow failing institutions to be acquired despite a lack of adequate capital.

11. Inept supervision and a permissive attitude by the Federal Home Loan Bank Board during the 1980s allowed badly managed and insolvent savings and loans to continue to operate.

12. Delayed closure of insolvent savings and loans compounded the FSLIC's losses.

13. Regulators hid the accumulating losses from the public.

14. Congressional delays and inaction, due to an unwillingness to confront the true size of the savings and loan debacle, prevented appropriate action.

15. Flip flops on real estate tax actions led to a boom/bust in the industry.

Although each of these causes played a role in the collapse of the thrift industry, the change in tax incentives was a major part of the problem. The accelerated depreciation allowed by the Economic Recovery Tax Act of 1981 increased investment in new construction financed by thrifts. The Tax Equity and Fiscal Responsibility Act of 1982 and the Deficit Reduction Tax Act of 1984 substantially reduced these benefits, but the Tax Reform Act of 1986 had the largest impact on the construction boom, as investors were no longer allowed to use passive losses to offset active income. Closing the tax shelter loophole was a huge blow to the construction industry and to institutions that had funded the boom with aggressive lending.

Selected Statistics, FSLIC-Insured Savings and Loans, 1980–1989 ($ Billions)

Year	Number of S&Ls	Total Assets	Net Income	Tangible Capital	Tangible Capital/ Total Assets	No. Insolvent S&Ls	Assets in Insolvent S&Ls	FSLIC Reserves
1980	3,993	$604	$0.8	$32	5.3%	43	$0.4	$6.5
1981	3,751	640	-4.6	25	4.0	112	28.5	6.2
1982	3,287	686	-4.1	4	0.5	415	220.0	6.3
1983	3,146	814	1.9	4	0.4	515	284.6	6.4
1984	3,136	976	1.0	3	0.3	695	360.2	5.6
1985	3,246	1,068	3.7	8	0.8	705	358.3	4.6
1986	3,220	1,162	0.1	14	1.2	672	343.1	-6.3
1987	3,147	1,249	-7.8	9	0.7	672	353.8	-13.7
1988	2,949	1,349	-13.4	22	1.6	508	297.3	-75.0
1989	2,878	1,252	-17.6	10	0.8	516	290.8	NA

Source: An Examination of the Banking Crises of the 1980s and Early 1990s

Besides the savings and loan crisis, the economy was constrained by several imbalances that had accumulated over the prior two decades. Some of these imbalances were concentrated in specific sectors or regions of the country, but with effects generally felt nationwide. Demographic trends that had boosted household formation faded quickly. The formation rate jumped to 2.5 percent in the 1970s, from 1.8 percent in the 1960s. It slipped to 1.7 percent from 1983 to 1989, before falling to just 0.8 percent between 1989 and 1991. Private debt built up at a rapid rate—from 1982 to 1988, and household debt increased at a 12 percent annual rate. Relative to income, debt grew at a 7 percent rate, while corporate borrowing surged by 11 percent. Mortgage-related borrowing surged by 12 percent per year over this period, and commercial real estate borrowing increased at a 10 percent annual rate. As such, residential and commercial real estate showed signs of overbuilding, by the late 1980s. Vacancy rates in rental housing rose to almost 8 percent by 1987, from a cycle low of 5 percent, and the commercial vacancy rate doubled to 16 percent by 1988.

Financial imbalances beyond the savings and loan industry were also evident, as large money center banks had accumulated a large balance of non-performing loans made to third-world countries, especially in Latin America. This led to a more cautious approach to lending in general that helped slow the economy. Defense spending was also cut when fiscal priorities shifted as the Cold War drew to a close. Real defense purchases of goods and services fell by 4 percent between 1987 and 1990, after having surged by 60 percent between 1979 and 1987. The defense downsizing led to the planned closing of fifty facilities in 1989, and the resulting dislocation played a role in dragging the economy into the 1990–1991 recession.

Like all postwar cycles, the lagged effects of monetary policy decisions and the level of long-term interest rates played significant roles in bringing about the recession. For this recession, solid economic growth in both 1987 and 1988 pushed capacity utilization rates up substantially, and the unemployment rate fell to its lowest level in fifteen years. The 1986 collapse in crude oil prices was a key factor in boosting real economic activity over the next two years. Saudi Arabia's decision to grab market share back from OPEC members who had been producing above their quotas caused crude oil prices to tumble to $12 per barrel in 1984.

The upturn in the economy late in the cycle spurred concerns that the economy might be outstripping its productive capacity, increasing the possibility of rising inflation. As a result, the Federal Reserve attempted to engineer a soft landing, by preemptively hiking rates. The federal funds rate was boosted by some 235 basis points in 1988 to end the year slightly over 9 percent. This uptick in rates continued into June 1989 when the funds rate peaked at 10.48 percent. The 10-year Treasury note rose by almost 210 basis points over this period to peak at 9.14 percent in December 1998. Long rates remained elevated right through the beginning of the recession in March 1990, even though the federal funds rate retraced most of its increase prior to the start of the consolidation in activity.

Chapter 10

The March 2001–November 2001 9/11 Recession

The eight-month contraction in the economy in 2001 was unusually mild—so mild, in fact, that the National Bureau of Economic Research (NBER) took about as long as the recession lasted, to declare that a consolidation had begun. Moreover, it was not until July 2003 that the organization determined that the recovery had begun in November 2001. The uniqueness of this recession is evident in the fact that this was the first postwar downturn where the NBER did not assert that the economy had returned to good health. Instead, the NBER highlighted the fact that employment had not begun to recover, even though real GDP had been rising for the past eighteen months, since November 2001. The early 2001 recession was the first postwar consolidation in which the elimination of high-paying jobs became a political issue.

The 2001 recession followed the longest expansion of the postwar period. The March 1991 to March 2001 expansion lasted 120 months, (ten years). This period of prosperity witnessed the explosion of the Internet and the rapid assimilation of digital technology into all aspects of day-to-day life. It also powered a rapid advance in equity markets, and the associated upturn in wealth powered the second half of the expansion. The Dot-Com crash and the rapid loss of financial wealth is often touted as the cause behind the collapse of the Clinton expansion, but other important catalysts should not be ignored as potential causes. Other possible recession triggers include the following:

- The Asian Crisis of 1997 resulted in a surging trade deficit.
- Investment spending experienced a boom/bust associated with the Y2K craze.
- The Fed hiked rates six times between June 1999 and May 2000 to temper growth.
- Enron's bankruptcy and other accounting scandals damaged investor confidence.
- The United States was the target of terror attacks on September 11, 2001.

Of all the possible causes of the recession, the corporate balance sheet restructuring associated with the Enron situation was more responsible for the recession than the bursting of the Dot-Com Bubble. The liquidity crises triggered by the forced balance sheet restructuring of the nonfinancial corporate sector resulted in a rapid shift in expectations and a consolidation in the economy. The speed at which markets accommodated this restructuring was critical in dampening the effect on the broader economy, making this a shallow recession.

The Fed's rapid response following the September 11 attacks also helped limit the contraction in activity. The funds rate was cut by 450 basis points between January and November 2001, to a level of just 2 percent. Additionally, the Clinton budget surplus made it easy for the George W. Bush team to rush through a tax cut to further limit the downturn, even though much of the tax cut was saved and not spent.

The tenth recession of the postwar period was mild by most macroeconomic measures. The recession was somewhat shorter than usual, and was concentrated in the third quarter of 2001. In fact, for the full year, real GDP rose by 0.2 percent, whereas the average decline during a recession is 1.9 percent. The deepest downturn was 3.4 percent, according to current data, and the smallest, prior to 2001, was minus 0.14 percent. From a GDP accounting perspective, the 2001 contraction was concentrated in a decline in nonresidential fixed investment (minus 8.1 percent) split between equipment and structures, and a decline in exports (minus 10.04 percent). Statistically, recessions that follow long expansions tend to be mild, and the 2001 experience is no exception. Even the decline in employment was relatively mild, with less than a 1 percent decline compared to a postwar average of 2.2 percent. The consolidation, however, did lead to the permanent loss of high-paying jobs, as the investment boom that preceded the bust was concentrated in labor-saving new equipment. This helps explain why the labor recovery was so shallow that it took a full year and a half to determine that the recession had ended.

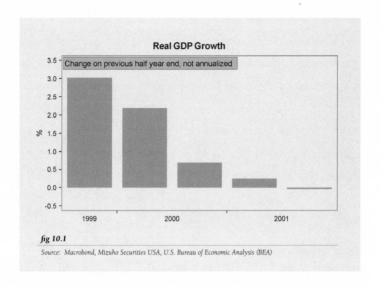

fig 10.1

Source: Macrobond, Mizuho Securities USA, U.S. Bureau of Economic Analysis (BEA)

The boom/bust in investment spending is the most widely recognized driver of the economy under the Clinton-Bush period. The run-up to Y2K and the growth of the World Wide Web, beginning in 1993 with the release of the Mosaic web browser, powered the economy during the March 1991– March 2001 expansion. During this ten-year period, investment in information processing equipment and software grew from around 17 percent of corporate spending on business fixed investment in the late 1970s, to more than 35 percent in the mid-2000s. From 1990 to 1995, spending on information processing and software grew by a little more than 12 percent per year. From 1995 to 2000, this GDP investment category surged by 19 percent per year on average. As a result, equipment and software investment directly added about 1 percent to quarterly real GDP of 4 percent, up from just 0.3 percent of average growth of 2.3 percent.

Beginning in the second half of 2000, businesses began scaling back their purchases of most types of capital goods, including high-tech equipment and software. Over the four quarters of 2001, real business fixed investment in information processing equipment and software fell 9 percent. This subtracted 0.3 percent from 2001 real GDP, cutting the growth in the economy in half. With so sharp a swing in growth coming from investment spending, and a deduction in exports due to the strong dollar, the Fed's fears of inflation proved unfounded, and the rising short-rate environment led to rising real rates. The consumer price index rose by only 1.6 percent in 2001, with a 13 percent decline in energy, offsetting a small acceleration in the core CPI to 2.7 percent from its 2.3 percent recent average. Moreover, there was a real absence of price pressures in the production pipeline. The producer price index (PPI) for finished goods fell by 1.8 percent in the twelve months ending in December 2001.

What actually caused the recession is still a point of debate among economists, with some suggesting that its origins can be traced back to the Asian financial crisis that began in May 1997. The Russian financial crisis and the failure of Long-Term Capital Management in September 1998 are also seen as possible causes of the recession. Alternatively, many macroeconomists see the bursting of the Dot-Com Bubble as the cause of the downturn. The NASDAQ peaked on March 10, 2000, and subsequently fell 78 percent over the following thirty months. The collapse in equities has been credited to six Fed rate hikes between June 1999 and May 2000 that were designed to rein

Real BFI Contributions to Real GDP Growth (Percentage Points)

	1970–79	1980–89	1990–95	1996–2000	2001
Real GDP Growth	3.3	3.0	2.3	4.0	0.3
Contributions from:					
Nonresidential fixed investment	0.6	0.4	0.4	1.2	-0.7
Structures	0.1	0.1	0.1	0.2	-0.1
Equipment and software	0.5	0.3	0.5	1.0	-0.6
Information processing	0.3	0.4	0.3	0.7	-0.3
Computers and peripherals	0.1	0.2	0.2	0.3	0.0
Software	0.0	0.1	0.1	0.2	0.0
Other	0.1	0.1	0.1	0.2	-0.2
Industrial equipment	0.1	0.0	0.0	0.1	-0.1
Transportation equipment	0.1	0.0	0.1	0.1	-0.2
Other	0.1	0.0	0.0	0.1	0.0

Source: Was Y2K Behind the Business Investment Boom and Bust, Federal Reserve Bank of St. Louis, 2003

in 4 percent growth and an inflation rate that had climbed to 3.4 percent from 2.7 percent in 1999. The federal funds rate was increased by 150 basis points to 6.5 percent; however, the implied real rate seems much too low to have caused a consolidation in the economy. Other factors credited with the downturn include the manipulation of the California electric industry and the resulting rise in energy prices, along with rolling blackouts, and the September 11 terror attacks. In reality, the attacks in New York and Virginia primarily amplified the contraction experienced during the third quarter of 2001.

The Asian financial crisis began in Thailand in May 1997 when the Thai baht (Thai currency) was hit by massive speculative selling. The country's currency peg left it vulnerable as its economy downshifted from a record 9 percent per year growth, from 1985 to 1996. The government's inability to maintain the peg led the prime minister to abruptly float the baht on July 2, 1997. A rapid devaluation followed, and financial markets in the region went into a tailspin. The resulting collapse in confidence and market illiquidity pushed debt-to-GDP ratios from 100 percent to 167 percent in the four largest Asian countries. The International Monetary Fund (IMF) eventually had to step in with a $40 billion currency stabilization program before the crisis began to abate that August.

The October 27, 1997, mini stock market crash was directly tied to the Asian crisis, even though the Asian "flu" had begun to ease. The Dow Jones Industrial Average began to decline at the opening bell, following the lead of overseas markets. The Hong Kong's Hang Seng Index was down 6 percent overnight, leading to declines in Europe and finally in the United States. When the markets opened for business in New York, the Dow quickly declined by 350 points, triggering a temporary halt in trading. Later that day, the industrial average fell another 550 points, triggering a second temporary halt in trading. The decline over the session is still the fifteenth largest percentage loss in the index since its creation in 1896. The circuit breakers appeared to have worked even though trading had been halted for the day, as the last halt had happened close to the normal end of the business day.

Following quickly on the heels of the Asian crisis and the mini-crash, came the Russian financial crisis of 1998 and the associated failure of Long-Term Capital Management. The ruble crisis hit on August 17, 1998, after the Russian central bank devalued the currency and defaulted on its debt. The hedge fund founded by legendary Salomon Brothers trader John Meriwether, and run with the help of Nobel Prize–winning economists Myron S. Scholes and Robert C. Merton, suffered a $4.6 billion trading loss in options on Russian debt and had to be bailed out by regulators. This combination of financial accidents could have resulted in a recession; however, the response by quick-thinking policymakers limited the aftereffects, and the market adjusted quickly with little damage to the real economy.

Corporate balance sheet deterioration is the least flashy explanation for the 2001 recession, but the forced restructuring of corporate liabilities that coincided with the downturn in the economy is the most likely cause of the consolidation. The failure of several high-profile companies like Enron, World-Com, and Calpine as a result of creative accounting, fraud, and collusion with auditors brought into question the financial health of many important companies. This prompted the passage of the Sarbanes-Oxley Act in 2002, and shifted the risk from shareholders to management for fraudulent practices and accounting errors.

The recession proved to be fairly short and mild, in part due to the accommodative policies adopted by the Federal Reserve before and after the terrorist attacks that quickly restored confidence in the financial markets. The Fed had sensed that monetary policy had unnecessarily tightened reserve market conditions as the anticipated inflation acceleration failed to materialize, and concerns had mounted regarding the markets' freeze in the aftermath of the September 11 attacks. As such, the Federal Reserve under Chairman Alan Greenspan cut short-term rates eleven times in 2001, to end

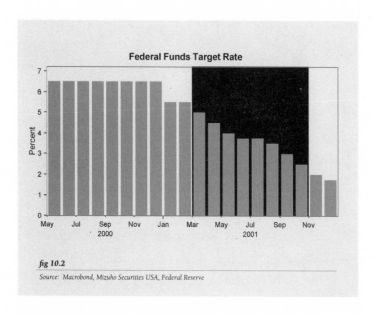

fig 10.2

Source: *Macrobond, Mizuho Securities USA, Federal Reserve*

the year at just 1.75 percent. The Fed maintained an accommodative policy stance through all of 2002 and 2003, and cut rates to 1 percent before the easing was ended.

Fulfilling a campaign promise to stimulate the economy, even though the NBER had not yet declared a recession, the George W. Bush administration pushed a sizable tax cut through Congress that also helped minimize the downturn in the economy and accelerated the corporate balance sheet restructuring. The Economic Growth and Tax Relief Reconciliation Act of 2001 became law in June 2001, shortly before the terrorist attacks. The retroactive nature of many of the cuts led to increased household and corporate liquidity early enough to help offset the balance sheet factors leading to the contraction. The act included nine key tax adjustments:

1. Doubled the child tax credit from $500 to $1,000

2. Expanded the earned income tax credit

3. Provided greater deductions for education expenses and savings

4. Reduced the gift tax

5. Phased out estate and generation-skipping transfer taxes to be eliminated in 2010

6. Reduced the marriage penalty by doubling the standard deduction for married couples

7. Eliminated the planned phase-out of personal exemption for those earning more than $150,000 and phased down itemized deductions for those earning more than $100,000

8. Provided relief from the alternative minimum tax

9. Reduced tax rates—39.6 percent fell to 35 percent, 36 percent to 33 percent, 31 percent to 28 percent, 28 percent to 25 percent—and created a new 10 percent rate for those who paid 15 percent

Chapter 11

The December 2007–June 2009 Subprime Recession

The contraction in the economy that started in September 2007 and lasted until June 2009 is known as the Great Recession. The economic downturn lasted eighteen months, far exceeding the average duration. The economy shed 8.4 million jobs, (6.1 percent of all payroll employment). This was the largest loss in employment of any downturn since the Great Depression. By comparison, the deep 1981 recession resulted in only about half as many job losses. Even after the economy bottomed out in June 2009, the recovery remained anemic through 2015, forcing the Federal Reserve to hold short rates at near zero until December 16, 2015, when it hiked rates for the first time since 2006.

Real GDP contracted by 4.3 percent during the recession, while the civilian jobless rate peaked at 10 percent in October 2009. The financial effects of the Great Recession were also atypically deep, as home prices fell by some 30 percent, and the broad equity index, the S&P 500, fell 57 percent from its October 2007 peak to its March 2009 low. It is estimated that households lost about $14 trillion in wealth as a result of the decline in home and equity prices.

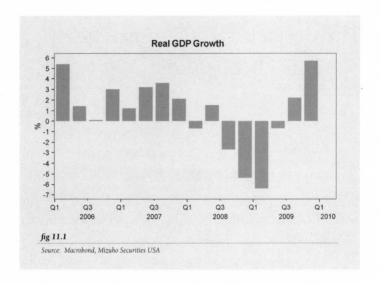

fig 11.1

Source: Macrobond, Mizuho Securities USA

An important aspect of the long and deep 2007–2009 recession was that it was the third downturn in the economy that was not the result of a Fed tightening cycle. Rate hikes did contribute to the problem confronting the economy by exposing the bubble-like conditions in the housing market. The bursting of that bubble led not only to a collapse in liquidity in the mortgage market, but also to illiquidity in other markets—especially the commercial paper market. The distress in the domestic housing market also pulled the global economy down, as many overseas investors had bought into the US housing bubble, and experienced their own liquidity crisis as bank capital was eaten up in losses on housing-related assets. The crisis saw the receivership of Fannie Mae and Freddie Mac, a government bailout of American International Group Inc. (AIG), and the failure of both Bear Stearns and Lehman Brothers.

To combat the combination of deteriorated household and banking industry balance sheets brought about by the bursting of the housing bubble, the Fed cut rates to near zero. The Fed was forced to execute a number of nontraditional initiatives to increase monetary policy accommodation, including targeted credit facilities and quantitative easing. The government also directly infused billions into financial and nonfinancial institutions to help turn the economy around and keep an anemic recovery going for several years until self-sustainability could be assured.

The bursting of the housing bubble was the principal contributor to the recession, but other considerations can't be ignored, including the downshift in defense spending as President Obama unwound US involvement in Iraq, and the Fed kept nominal short rates high, despite a lack of inflation. The terror attacks of September 11 caused US military involvement in Afghanistan to root out the Taliban, culminating in the initiative by President George W. Bush to topple the government of Saddam Hussein in Iraq. Operation Iraq Freedom lasted from March to May 2003, but winning peace proved to be much more difficult. As such, the US military got caught up in a protracted and expensive peacekeeping exercise that boosted defense spending to 4.8 percent of real GDP by 2007, up from 3.8 percent in 2000. Despite this increase, the rate of growth of defense spending slowed under President Obama as he removed troops from Iraq. This slowing in defense spending played a role in the recession by helping to expose the problems in the housing market.

National Defense Expenditures

	Defense Expenditures (Billions of Dollars)	Change in Defense from Previous Year (Billions of Dollars)	Defense as a Percentage of Gross Domestic Product (percent)
2000	370.3	9.7	3.8
2001	392.6	22.3	3.9
2002	437.1	44.5	4.2
2003	497.2	60.1	4.5
2004	550.7	53.5	4.7
2005	588.1	37.4	4.7
2006	624.1	36.0	4.7
2007	662.2	38.1	4.8

Source: BEA, Department of Commerce, Recession Prevention Handbook, Norman Frumkin, 2010

The low level of short-term interest rates maintained by the Greenspan Fed, through the first three years of the expansion that began in November 2001, has been cited as a key reason that the housing market bubble inflated. However, the steady rise in rates, beginning June 2004, from a low of just 1 percent to 5.25 percent in June 2006, was also a contributor to the bursting of the housing bubble. The Fed hiked rates and kept them high, despite the fact that inflation remained exceptionally mild, over the course of the six-year expansion. The headline CPI ranged from a low of 1.6 percent in 2002, to a high of just 3.4 percent in 2005. The following year, the headline CPI drifted down to 3.2 percent, and then to 2.8 percent in 2007 as short rates remained unchanged at 5.25 percent. This resulted in a rising real short-rate environment that began to squeeze the economy as regulators and rating agencies were pressured to get tough due to news stories of excessive speculation in the housing market.

It is easy to identify the reasons why the housing bubble inflated and why it burst. The seeds of the housing bubble go as far back as 1980, when regulations controlling bank mergers and interest rates paid on deposits were abolished. Banks, in 1982, were also allowed to offer adjustable rate mortgages, which became the flash point for the crisis. Capital gains rules that were applied to home sales were altered in 1997, increasing the exclusion to $500,000 for a married couple, and $250,000 for a single person, once every two years. Finally, in 1999, the Depression-era restriction on banks owning investment banks was eliminated. But the government's contribution to the housing bubble did not end there. The increasing requirement by both the Community Reinvestment Act and the Department of Housing and Urban Development (HUD) for government-sponsored enterprises to help stimulate affordable housing forced both Fannie Mae and Freddie Mac to steadily reduce underwriting standards on the loans they purchased in order to meet the new quotas. This situation would have industry-wide ramifications.

Historically low interest rates on mortgages resulted from the Fed's successful campaign to lower, and then anchor, inflation expectations. This made homes more affordable and led to rising home prices. In the wake of the Dot-Com crash, mortgage rates fell to an all-time low of 5.25 percent, from 8 percent for fixed-rate 30-year loans. Adjustable-rate loans also tumbled. A one-year adjustable-rate mortgage fell to a range of 3–4 percent from 7 percent a few years earlier. Lower rates allowed a larger share of the population to afford a home. As rates moved lower, and affordability rose, the percentage of households owning a home expanded. In 1994, 64 percent of households owned a home. By 2004, homeownership rate had risen to 69.2 percent.

As originators began to lower lending standards and documentation requirements, home prices rose. This easing of standards was undertaken by banks to increase market share in the lucrative market for new-issue mortgages. The rapidly expanding derivatives market further increased the demand for new-issue mortgages as collateral. Investors seeking higher yielding assets in contrast to the exceptionally low Treasury rate environment looked increasingly at derivatives to meet return requirements.

Inappropriate risk management tools and incorrect credit quality analysis by the rating agencies amplified the bubble, creating the appearance that new and riskier assets were safer than they proved to be. This was especially true regarding the booming market for subprime mortgages. A speculative aspect was also present in the housing bubble, as rising home prices led to investors buying homes just to flip them as prices kept climbing, especially in states like Arizona, Nevada, Florida, New York, New Jersey, and California. As a result, the S&P Case-Shiller 20-City Composite Home Price Index rose by 150 percent between 2002 and 2006, roughly 30 percent per year.

All bubbles burst, and the US housing bubble was no exception; however, identifying the factors that brought about the downturn was impossible in real time. Those who tried shorting the market in the run-up to the crisis lost money repeatedly, adding to the sense that the increase in home prices was unstoppable. As such, when the bubble burst in the wake of rising defaults, it caught households with too much real estate and related debt, off guard. The collapse in prices left many homeowners and real estate speculators upside down with negative equity. In such an abnormal position, owners of these properties walked away from their home or investment property, instead of struggling to remain solvent. The pace of defaults accelerated rapidly, resulting in banks getting caught with a rapidly rising portfolio of nonperforming loans. This then exacerbated the losses in the banking industry when banks pulled back liquidity, as their accumulating losses ate into their capital. The result was a more than 30 percent decline in home prices, from their peak, and a $14 trillion loss in household wealth.

The distress evident in both the household sector and the banking industry balance sheets was reflected in credit spreads as financial institutions began to fail. As the number and size

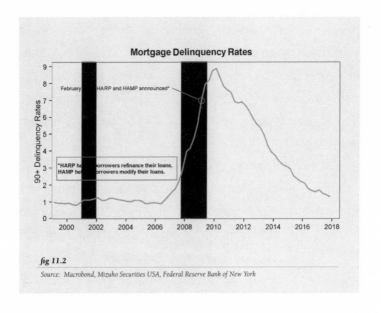

Mortgage Delinquency Rates

February   HARP and HAMP annnounced*

*HARP he[ ]orrowers refinance their loans,
HAMP he[ ]orrowers modify their loans.

fig 11.2

Source: Macrobond, Mizuho Securities USA, Federal Reserve Bank of New York

of failed institutions which were in trouble rose, questions about the government's ability to handle the situation, let alone during a transfer of power in the executive branch, added to the uncertainty and exacerbated the situation. The damage from the bursting of the US housing bubble spread from households to banks, and their investment banking arms, to investors such as insurance companies. Most notably, Bear Stearns, Lehman Brothers, and AIG saw their capital being eaten up by losses on their inventory of mortgage-related products, and in their proprietary trading activities. The attractive yields offered by derivatives using mortgages as collateral had attracted overseas investors, as well, during the bubble inflation phase, and broadened the crisis into a truly global problem. For a time, it looked as if a cycle of declining home prices, increasing mortgage defaults, and eroding bank capital would continue unabated. However, the Fed and the Treasury employed a host of innovative policy tools, under their emergency power, to eventually get ahead of the situation, and conditions began to stabilize.

Monetary policymakers' response to the crisis would evolve, but conditions deteriorated after the Treasury suspended the dividend on Fannie Mae's and Freddie Mac's preferred stock, on September 7, 2008. These policymakers had to travel down several nontraditional avenues to attack the problem, but only after more traditional tools had proven unsuccessful in dealing with the broadening crisis.

The Fed's initial response was to cut short-term rates, in an effort to keep liquidity flowing in the economy. Between September 2007 and December 2008, the makers of monetary policy cut the funds rate target from 5.25 percent, to a range of just 0.0–0.25 percent. Much of this reduction occurred between January and March 2008. These rate cuts were followed by the Federal Open Market Committee's first nontraditional policy tool—transmitting its policy intention through explicit forward guidance. The committee first suggested that rates would stay low for an extended period. This forward-looking policy guidance evolved further into specific calendar guidance. That August, the committee announced that rates would stay exceptionally low, at least through mid-2013. It wasn't until December 2015 that rates began to rise, even though the Fed had warned of a potential policy shift a year earlier.

Besides forward guidance, the Fed pursued two other nontraditional policy avenues during the Great Recession. The first were target policies designed to address specific liquidity issues between December 2007 and October 2008. These liquidity-specific programs were followed in November 2008 with a more general liquidity infusion provided by the Fed's large-scale asset purchase program that evolved through several phases, and eventually pushed the system's balance sheet to a $4.5 trillion peak in October 2014.

These efforts began to pay off by early 2009 when the economy expanded by 2.2 percent in the second quarter, and then by 5.7 percent in the third quarter. The recovery phase was atypically shallow, however, as growth quickly settled on a 2.25 percent growth trajectory, and employment growth proved to be unusually tepid. The constraints on credit that were brought about after the crisis were slowly reversed, and the recovery began to take hold. New regulations designed to avoid another repeat of the housing bubble constrained lending during the recovery, and tempered growth as companies focused on improving earnings and not growing their businesses.

NONTRADITIONAL MONETARY AND
FISCAL POLICIES IMPLEMENTED

Targeted Credit Facilities: The Fed established the term "auction facility" in December 2007, to provide term discount window loans to depository institutions. Liquidity swap arrangements were also authorized in that month to help overseas banks with short-term dollar funding, and the term securities lending facility was designed to help primary dealers with funding their holding of securities. The primary dealers credit facility was established in March 2008, and the asset-backed commercial paper money market mutual fund liquidity facility was established days after the Lehman Brothers failure. Finally, the commercial paper funding facility was announced in early October 2008.

Large-Scale Asset Purchase Programs: When short-term interest rates are already at their effective lower boundary, the Fed can inject liquidity into the economy by buying longer-term assets, lowering rates further out on the yield curve, and hopefully, providing a floor under inflation. In November 2008, the Fed announced that it would buy US agency mortgage-backed securities, as well as government-sponsored enterprise debt. This initiative was dubbed quantitative easing (QE). The initial QE plan was to buy $500 billion in agency mortgage-backed securities, and up to $100 billion in agency debt. This program was expanded in March 2009 to include $300 billion in long-term Treasury debt. Following its first asset purchase program, the Fed announced QE2 in November 2010, indicating it would buy an additional $600 billion in long-term Treasury securities by second quarter of 2011. It then launched Operation Twist in September 2011, when the Federal Open Market Committee announced it would sell short-term debt and buy longer duration assets to drive down long rates. QE3 was announced in

September 2012 as an open-ended purchase program of $40 billion a month, of agency mortgage-backed securities. By December 2012, the Fed upped the size of the open-ended program by $45 billion a month, with additional purchases of Treasury debt. QE3 or QE Infinity, as it was often called, lasted until December 2013 when the Fed began to taper its purchases by $10 billion a month. The Fed did not begin to reduce the size of its portfolio until the fourth quarter of 2016.

Fiscal Policy Response: The fiscal policy response took a little while to get organized, but on October 3, 2008, Congress passed the George W. Bush team's Troubled Asset Relief Program. This legislation provided up to $700 billion for the purchase of distressed assets and for capital infusions into financial institutions. Although this program was split into two equal installments of $350 billion, and the second phase required presidential notification to Congress and an affirmative vote by both houses, the program provided an immediate capital infusion into banks, through the purchase of preferred stock. The second installment was released in early January 2009, after President-elect Obama asked then-President Bush to notify Congress of the need to release the final $350 billion. Beyond this, fiscal policy was focused on assuring that a similar financial crisis in the future, would no longer require taxpayer funding.

Summary

Postwar Business Cycles in Brief

The following is a brief description of each of the postwar cycles. This can be used as a quick reference to the primary drivers of each recession, as a more detailed analysis of the associated financial debacles is reviewed.

1. **November 1948 to October 1949—First Postwar Recession**: Returning veterans swelled the workforce, and joblessness rose. The government's handling of the process was limited, as policymakers were more worried about inflation than unemployment.

2. **July 1953 to May 1954—Post–Korean War Recession**: A postwar pop in inflation was followed by increased defense spending, and the Fed hiked rates, due to growing concerns about inflation. The spike in rates led to increased pessimism and decreased aggregate demand.

3. **August 1957 to April 1958—Eisenhower Recession**: The Fed hiked rates and maintained them for an extended period, to contain inflation. This led to an appreciation in the US dollar, and a rising trade deficit that eventually

combined with a global recession, to tip the domestic economy into a recession.

4. **April 1960 to February 1961—Rolling Adjustment Recession**: The economy experienced a number of sequential hits, and the shift to compact cars initiated a big inventory correction in the auto industry, causing the economy to contract.

5. **December 1969 to November 1970—Nixon Recession**: Monetary and fiscal policies designed to temper inflation dialed back liquidity too much, and the economy dipped.

6. **November 1973 to March 1975—Oil Crisis Recession**: A quadrupling of oil prices and high government spending on the Vietnam War led to stagflation, and the unemployment rate reached 9 percent in May 1975.

7. **January to July 1980—Carter Credit-Control Recession**: Inflation spiked to 13.5 percent, and the White House implemented credit controls. The disruptive nature of these controls led to a liquidity squeeze and a quick downturn in the economy.

8. **July 1981 to November 1982—Iranian Energy Crisis Recession**: US embassy officials were taken hostage in Tehran by an Islamic cleric–led revolution that had overthrown the US-backed Shah, and this resulted in substantially higher energy prices. The inflation rate quickly reflected this, and the prior energy market shock. The evolution of a wage and price spiral prompted the Volcker Fed to tighten aggressively, and the prime rates (rates that banks charge preferred customers) climbed to 21.5 percent in 1982.

9. **July 1990 to March 1991—Gulf War Recession**: Iraq invaded Kuwait, and another rise in oil prices caused manufacturing to contract even as the North American Free Trade Agreement (NAFTA) made the moving of facilities to Canada and Mexico more attractive. The equity market crashed after the failed leveraged buyout of United Airlines, by its unions, which compounded the credit crisis that was triggered by the collapse of the savings and loan industry.

10. **March to November 2001—The 9/11 Recession**: The collapse of the Dot-Com Bubble, the terrorist attacks of September 11, and accounting scandals at major US companies contributed to a recession that was cut short by aggressive counter cyclical fiscal and monetary policy response.

11. **December 2007 to June 2009—Subprime Recession**: Rising default rates on derivative investments tied to the housing market caused two Bear Stearns–owned hedge funds to fail. The resulting reverberations caused the government to bail out several banks and financial institutions. The associated deterioration in household balance sheets, on the back of declining home prices, led to a deep and protracted recession.

The variation in duration and depth of these eleven postwar downturns stems from several factors. Oil prices, which were a key determinant in at least four business cycles, the expansion and contraction in defense spending, along with inflation concerns, and the associated monetary policy tightening were the primary drivers of business cycles, prior to 1990. These cycles tended to be punctuated by isolated financial market dislocations, which were typically the failure of one key bank or financial institution. The last three recessions, however, have involved the dislocation of an entire industry or sector (e.g., the savings and loan industry, the nonfinancial corporate sector, or the household sector/financial services industry). Policy mistakes, from regulatory and counter-cyclical monetary, to fiscal, continued to play a role in each of these cycles, but more as a catalyst for the accumulating financial imbalances in the economy to surface. This changed dynamic will become clearer in the detailed discussion of business cycle and financial dislocations that follows.

Evolution of Financial Debacles

Financial debacles (crises) are often associated with business cycles, and more recently they have become the catalyst behind downturns in the economy. The two most important financial dislocations in the history of the United States are the devastating collapse of US stocks on Black Tuesday, October 29, 1929, and the bursting of the housing bubble in 2007, along with the subprime crisis that followed. Both events were associated with a system-wide banking crisis and debt-related deflation pressures. The 1929 incident heralded in the Great Depression, while the events of 2007 triggered the Great Recession. Both financial crises led to major changes in the regulatory structure, intended to safeguard the economy from systemic financial dislocations. The Banking Act of 1933, generally referred to as Glass-Steagall, rewrote the banking laws to separate commercial banks from investment banks, and restrict other speculative banking activities employed by commercial banks. It restored commercial banking to its role defined in the Federal Reserve Act of 1913. Glass-Steagall also created the Federal Deposit Insurance Corporation (FDIC) and established Regulation Q that set a cap on the interest rates that banks could pay on deposits. This legislation also created the Federal Open Market Committee, and charged the Federal Reserve with an expanded regulatory role and responsibility for macro developments.

The 2007 financial market crisis led to the passage of the Wall Street Reform and Consumer Protection Act of 2010, also know as Dodd-Frank. This legislative initiative increased the amount of capital that banks must hold in reserve to provide an added cushion against loan losses. It also required banks to keep a larger portion of their assets invested in things that can be easily liquidated in the event of a run on a bank's deposits. All banks with more than $50 billion worth of assets on their balance sheets must submit to annual stress tests, adminis-tered by the Federal Reserve, designed to see if the bank could survive a crisis scenario. Banks determined to be global sys-temically important (G-SIBs) required an additional tranche of capital referred to as the G-SIB surcharge. Proprietary trading by broker-dealers was also eliminated under the Volcker Rule portion of the legislation, limiting trading to serve as market makers for institutional clients. Finally, the Consumer Finan-cial Protection Bureau was founded, and charged with protect-ing consumers from deceptive and abusive financial products and services.

Interpretations of what caused the Great Depression range from the traditional Keynesian view of a collapse in aggregate demand to the monetarist focus on the 35 percent contraction in money. More recently, the role of debt deflation has been identified as the cause of the Great Depression. The concept is basically that loose credit standards led to overindebtedness, fueling speculation and asset bubbles that caused a collapse in credit and the banking system when the bubble burst. Throughout the entirety of the Great Depression, it is estimated that more than nine thousand US banks failed—by far the worst stretch in domestic history regarding bank failures. The debt deflation interpretation of the Great Depression coincides with the meltdown experienced between 2007 and 2009. A bubble in home prices resulted in an explosion in debt that fueled the bubble, and when defaults picked up, the collapse brought down the banking industry and damaged the household sector's balance sheet.

The importance of these two banking crises frames our analysis of postwar business cycles and the evolution of financial dislocations associated with them. Analyzing each cycle and how banks fared through the downturn leads to an important conclusion. Specifically, the nature of the credit cycle associated with recessions has changed, beginning with the 1990–1991 recession, from those experienced over the prior forty years. The latest three business cycles, in fact, have been led or amplified by a forced restructuring of a key macro balance sheet. These include the collapse of the thrift industry, the restructuring of the nonfinancial corporate balance sheet, and more recently, the collapse of the banking industry, and the deterioration in the household balance sheet.

Federal Deposit Insurance Corporation Failures and Assistance Transactions
(Dollar Amounts in Thousands) 1947–1949 Recession

Institution Name	Location	Effective Date	Ins. Fund	Transaction Type*	Failure / Assistance	Total Deposits	Total Assets
Farmers Merchants State Bank	Spencerville, IN	10/8/49	FDIC	P&A	FAILURE	437	354
The Citizens Banking Company	Weston, OH	6/11/49	FDIC	P&A	FAILURE	742	740
Stockmens Bank of Martinsdale	Martinsdale, MT	4/30/49	FDIC	P&A	FAILURE	709	634
The First National Bank of Dyer	Dyer, IN	2/19/49	FDIC	P&A	FAILURE	3,090	3,157
The First State Bank	Franklin, TX	12/18/48	FDIC	P&A	FAILURE	609	694
The American National Bank of Pryor Creek	Pryor, OK	11/20/48	FDIC	P&A	FAILURE	1,925	1,774
Columbus Trust Company	Newark, NJ	7/24/48	FDIC	P&A	FAILURE	7,921	7,892
*Purchase and Assumption							

Source: FDIC HSOB Bank & Thrift Failures, 1947–1949

The financial dislocations between these two systemic collapses (1929–1933 and 2007–2009) range from simple one-off local bank failures, caused by check fraud or embezzlement, to the collapse of a major regional bank in the wake of fraud and declining energy prices, to the near collapse of a money center bank on the back of bad emerging market loans. Besides banks, the Asian and Russian financial crises precipitated the failure of a major hedge fund that eventually required recapitalization from sixteen major global financial institutions, orchestrated by Fed Chairman Alan Greenspan and Treasury Secretary Robert Rubin. In this section, we identify the bank failures associated with each downturn in the economy to understand the important role that banks played in each of the postwar business cycles.

Early postwar recessions (1948 to 1970) were inflation cycles dominated by excess demand that resulted in a contractionary monetary policy. Each of these business cycles was associated with a number of bank failures, but most were the result of fraud and embezzlement, such as an accumulation of bad checks or misappropriation of funds by bank employees, or inappropriate lending decisions. A few failures during this period were related to fraudulent securities transactions, but only three banks failed due to unsound lending practices. As such, financial dislocations were not a cause of the early postwar recession, nor directly caused by the downturn in the economy.

The second phase of postwar business cycles was also caused by policies designed to contain (rein in) inflation. The three cycles experienced between 1973 and 1982 were dominated by supply-side constraints, in contrast to the excess aggregate demand that led to the previous five recessions. A combination of repeated energy shocks and an aggressive program of credit controls caused the next series of downturns in the economy. One obvious indication that the economy and markets had begun to evolve over this ten-year period is evident in the number of financial institutions that failed in the wake of recession and the size of the institutions involved. The 1973–1975 recession resulted in twenty-three bank failures, the largest of which was Franklin National Bank of New York, which had $1.4 million in deposits and $3.7 million in assets. Twenty-two additional banks failed during the six-month January to July 1980 recession.

The largest bank to fail during the Carter credit crunch-induced recession was First Pennsylvania Bank of Philadelphia, which had $5 million in deposits and just under $8 million in assets at the time it failed. Bank failures spiked to 159 during the Reagan recession, which stretched from July 1981 to November 1982. Although the size of failed institutions was relatively small, compared to Franklin National and First Pennsylvania, the magnitude of the effect on the industry was huge, totaling almost $45 billion in deposits and $57.5 billion in assets. This evolution from isolated bank failures to bigger and more broad-based failures reflects the growing dependence on debt financing and the transition in the economy from one of aggregate demand, leading business cycles to supply constraints, causing inflation. Monetary and fiscal policies are well suited to deal with excess demand situations, but not with inflation induced by a supply shock.

Supply constraints proved to be a drag on underlying growth, and resulted in rising interest rates at both ends of the yield curve. Lower-trend growth and higher rates left companies searching for ways to boost their top line, and increased leverage was viewed as an easy way to reverse the growing malaise. This increased dependence on debt-related financing increased the role of credit in deterring how the business cycle evolved. In fact, the last three business cycles of the postwar period were credit-induced, not inflation-induced. The July 1990 to March 1991 recession resulted from the collapse of the thrift industry, while the March to November 2001 recession was caused by corporate malfeasance, which led to a forced restructuring of corporate balance sheets. The latest postwar cycle—the long, deep December 2007 to June 2009 recession—was the result of the housing bubble burst that crushed household balance sheets, and pulled the banking industry down with it. The evolution of financial dislocations from one-off events caused by recession to leading business cycles will be clearly evident, after reviewing the rich history of postwar financial debacles.

Chapter 12

Financial Dislocations and the Business Cycle

Financial market dislocations (crises) are often associated with business cycles, and have recently become the catalyst behind a downturn in the economy. The two most important historical dislocations for the US economy were the devastating collapse of US stocks on Black Tuesday, October 29, 1929, and the more recent subprime crisis initiated by the unwinding of investment bank Bear Stearns that began on June 22, 2007. These two events were associated with a system-wide banking crisis and debt deflation pressures. The 1929 incident heralded in the Great Depression, while the events of 2007 triggered the Great Recession. Both financial crises led to major changes in the regulatory structure, intended to safeguard the economy from systemic financial dislocations. The Banking Act of 1933, generally referred to as Glass-Steagall, rewrote the banking laws to separate commercial banks from investment banks, and restrict other speculative banking activities employed by commercial banks. It restored commercial banking to its role defined in the Federal Reserve Act of 1913. Glass-Steagall also created the Federal Deposit Insurance Corporation (FDIC) and established Regulation Q, which set a cap on the interest rates banks that could pay on deposits. This legislation also created the Federal Open Market Committee, and charged the Federal Reserve with an expanded regulatory role and responsibility for macro developments.

The 2007 financial market crisis led to the passage of the Wall Street Reform and Consumer Protection Act of 2010, also known as Dodd-Frank. This legislative initiative increased the amount of capital that banks must hold in reserve to provide an added cushion against loan losses. It also required banks to keep a larger portion of their assets invested in things that can be easily liquidated in the event of a run on a bank's deposits. All banks with more than $50 billion worth of assets on their balance sheets must submit to annual stress tests, administered by the Federal Reserve. The tests are designed to see if the bank could survive a crisis scenario. Banks determined to be global systemically important (G-SIBs) are required to hold an additional tranche of capital, referred to as the G-SIB surcharge. Proprietary trading by security firms was also eliminated under the Volcker Rule portion of the legislation, limiting trading to serving as market makers for institutional clients. Finally, the Consumer Financial Protection Bureau was founded, and charged with protecting consumers from deceptive and abusive financial products and services.

Interpretations of what caused the Great Depression range from the traditional Keynesian view of a collapse in aggregate demand to the monetarist focus on the 35 percent contraction in money. More recently, the role of debt deflation has been identified as the cause of the Great Depression. The concept is basically that loose credit standards led to overindebtedness, fueling speculation and asset bubbles that caused a collapse in credit and the banking system when the bubble burst. Throughout the entirety of the Great Depression, it is estimated that more than nine thousand US banks failed—by far the worst stretch in domestic history regarding bank failures. The debt deflation interpretation of the Great Depression coincides with the meltdown experienced between 2007 and 2009. A bubble in home prices resulted in an explosion in debt to fuel the bubble, and when defaults picked up, the collapse brought down the banking industry and damaged the household sector's balance sheet.

These two banking crises frame our postwar business cycles and the evolution of financial dislocations associated with them. Analyzing each cycle and how banks fared through the downturn leads to an important conclusion. Specifically, the nature of the credit cycle associated with recessions has changed, beginning with the 1990–1991 recession, from those experienced over the prior forty years. The latest three business cycles, in fact, have been led or amplified by a forced restructuring of a key macro sector balance sheet. These include the collapse of the thrift industry, the restructuring of the nonfinancial corporate balance sheet, and more recently, the collapse of the banking industry and the deterioration in the household balance sheet.

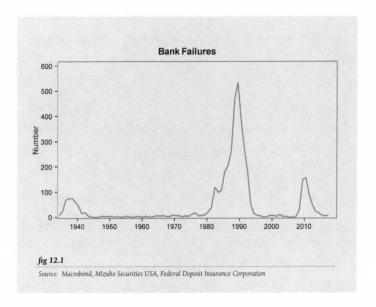

fig 12.1

Source: Macrobond, Mizuho Securities USA, Federal Deposit Insurance Corporation

The financial dislocations between these two systemic collapses (1929–1933 and 2007–2009) range from simple one-off local bank failures, caused by check fraud or embezzlement, to the collapse of a major regional bank in the wake of fraud and declining energy prices, to the near collapse of a money center bank on the back of bad, emerging market loans. Besides banks, the Asian and Russian financial crises precipitated the failure of a major hedge fund, which eventually required recapitalization from sixteen major global financial institutions, orchestrated by Fed Chairman Alan Greenspan and Treasury Secretary Robert Rubin. The next several chapters will review the history of bank failures associated with each downturn in the economy to understand the role banks played, if any, in each of the postwar business cycles.

Early postwar recessions (1948 to 1970) were inflation

cycles dominated by excess demand that resulted in a contractionary monetary policy. Each business cycle was associated with several bank failures, but most failures were the result of fraud and embezzlement, such as an accumulation of bad checks or misappropriation of funds by bank employees. A few failures during this period were related to fraudulent securities transactions, but only three banks failed due to unsound lending practices. As such, financial dislocations were not a cause of the early postwar recession nor directly caused by the downturn in the economy. They appear to have been simply side effects of what was transpiring in the broader economy.

The first recession of the postwar period, November 1948 to October 1949, was driven largely by returning veterans and the government's disappointing handling of the process. The result was a simple inventory and inflation-led contraction in the economy. Keynesian fiscal policy was employed to mitigate the recession, as the memory of the Great Depression loomed large in policymakers' consciousness. The result was a limited number of bank failures associated with the recession. Of the seven banks that failed during this period, the largest was Columbus Trust Company of Newark, New Jersey. The bank had $7.9 million in deposits, and fell victim to embezzlement totaling $657,000 on some twenty mortgages made on fictitious properties, most of which were apartment buildings. Embezzlement also brought down the American National Bank of Pryor Creek, Oklahoma. The fraudulent deposits totaled some $800,000 of the bank's $1.9 million in total deposits. The First National Bank of Dyer, Indiana, fell victim to more than $200,000 in bad checks, passed by a local used car dealer. These were noteworthy only because they coincided with the recession, not because they contributed in any significant way.

Federal Deposit Insurance Corporation Failures and Assistance Transactions (Dollar Amounts in Thousands) 1947–1949 Recession

Institution Name	Location	Effective Date	Ins. Fund	Transaction Type*	Failure / Assistance	Total Deposits	Total Assets
Farmers Merchants State Bank	Spencerville, IN	10/8/49	FDIC	P&A	FAILURE	437	354
The Citizens Banking Company	Weston, OH	6/11/49	FDIC	P&A	FAILURE	742	740
Stockmens Bank of Martinsdale	Martinsdale, MT	4/30/49	FDIC	P&A	FAILURE	709	634
The First National Bank of Dyer	Dyer, IN	2/19/49	FDIC	P&A	FAILURE	3,090	3,157
The First State Bank	Franklin, TX	12/18/48	FDIC	P&A	FAILURE	609	694
The American National Bank of Pryor Creek	Pryor, OK	11/20/48	FDIC	P&A	FAILURE	1,925	1,774
Columbus Trust Company	Newark, NJ	7/24/48	FDIC	P&A	FAILURE	7,921	7,892
*Purchase and Assumption							

Source: FDIC HSOB Bank & Thrift Failures, 1947–1949

The post–Korean War recession, July 1953 to May 1954, was a classic inflation cycle with increased defense spending leading to higher short rates and a contraction in aggregate demand. This second recession of the postwar period was again associated with a small increase in bank failures, but it was also due to one-off developments related to bad banking practices. Specifically, four banks failed during the recession, and the largest was the First State Bank of Elmwood Park, Illinois. The bank failed due to a combination of factors, including a scheme by its parent, Banker Discount Corp., to sell discount paper to First State Bank, and use the proceeds as capital in the bank. Extensive concentration of assets held in Banker Discount Corp. liabilities also ran afoul of state bank laws, in addition to accounting irregularities relating to a pool of funds accumulated for political contributions. The other three failed banks were taken down by an accumulation of bad checks or employees who misappropriated funds, which, when discovered, caused a capital and control problem for the banks. Rising rates and a dip in the economy may have played a factor in these developments, but there was no lasting macro effect from these bank failures.

Federal Deposit Insurance Corporation Failures and Assistance Transactions
(Dollar Amounts in Thousands) 1953–1954 Recession

Institution Name	Location	Effective Date	Ins. Fund	Transaction Type*	Failure / Assistance	Total Deposits	Total Assets
Bank of Whitesville	Whitesville, KY	10/1/54	FDIC	P&A	FAILURE	930	1,040
Bank of Ila	Ila, GA	8/9/54	FDIC	P&A	FAILURE	60	98
First State Bank of Elm-wood Park	Elmwood Park, IL	5/26/53	FDIC	P&A	FAILURE	16,957	17,456
*Purchase and Assumption							

Source: FDIC HSOB Bank & Thrift Failures, 1953

The Eisenhower recession was caused by high, short-term rates maintained for an extended period, resulting in a rising dollar, and a trade deficit that eventually combined with weaker global demand, to produce a recession. This third cycle of the postwar period saw five bank failures associated with the downturn in the economy. Three were the result of shortages discovered at the bank and blamed on employees. These were the First National Bank of Halfway, Oregon; First State Bank of Yorktown, Texas; and Rushville Banking Company of Ohio. These shortages ranged from as little as $100,000 to a reported $590,000. The Rushville Banking Company failure was the largest, by both assets and deposits. Bad checks totaling $150,000 were blamed for the shortage at Manufacturers Bank of Edgewater, New Jersey, while improper lending accounted for the failure of Peoples State Bank of Richland, Texas. The bad loans did not appear to be the result of fraud; this was the first failure that could be the result of the business cycle.

1957–1958 Recession Federal Deposit Insurance Company Failures and Assistance Transactions (Dollar Amounts in Thousands)

Institution Name	Location	Effective Date	Ins. Fund	Transaction Type*	Failure / Assistance	Total Deposits	Total Assets
The Manufacturers Bank of Edgewater	Edgewater, NJ	7/17/58	FDIC	PO	FAILURE	2,213	2,365
The Rushville Banking Company	Rushville, OH	5/26/58	FDIC	P&A	FAILURE	4,084	4,476
Peoples State Bank	Richland Springs, TX	5/5/58	FDIC	PO	FAILURE	574	618
The First National Bank of Halfway	Halfway, OR	3/17/58	FDIC	PO	FAILURE	1,368	1,446
First State Bank of Yorktown	Yorktown, TX	4/10/57	FDIC	PO	FAILURE	1,163	1,253

*Purchase, Assumption on Deposit Payout

Source: FDIC HSOB Bank & Thrift Failures, 1957–58

The fourth cycle of the postwar period in 1960–1961 was described as the rolling adjustment recession because the economy experienced several sequential hits to individual industries or sectors, with the auto industry eventually tipping the economy into a downturn. Auto manufacturers were forced into a sharp inventory correction after consumers shifted toward compact vehicles, leaving dealers with the wrong inventory mix. Although this downturn was not the shortest to date, it did follow the shortest expansion— just 24 months from the previous trough to its peak. As a result, only two banks failed around this recession. As for all but one of the bank failures already discussed, embezzlement and check fraud were again involved. The Sheldon National Bank of Sheldon, Iowa was shut down immediately when it was discovered that a director and assistant cashier had embezzled $2.1 million. The bank had $3.8 million in deposits, and $4.3 million in assets at the time it was closed by the FDIC. The Capitol Hill State Bank in Oklahoma was closed after a shortage of more than $1.5 million was discovered at the bank. At the time, its assets were $7.5 million, and its deposits were just short of $7 million. The few bank failures recorded probably had more to do with the fact that the short expansion made it harder to hide anomalies in bank accounts.

Federal Deposit Insurance Corporation Failures and
Assistance Transactions (Dollar Amounts in Thousands)
1960–1961 Recession

Institution Name	Location	Effective Date	Ins. Fund	Transaction Type*	Failure / Assistance	Total Deposits	Total Assets
The Sheldon National Bank	Sheldon, IA	1/16/61	FDIC	PO	FAILURE	3,884	4,365
*PO = Payout							

Source: FDIC HSOB Bank & Thrift Failures, April 1960–February 1961

Fiscal and monetary policy designed to dial back inflation caused the Nixon recession. The eleven-month downturn was preceded by a long, eight-year and ten-month expansion. The downturn began in December 1969, and ended in November 1970. Although the recession was of average length, it was on the deeper side for postwar downturns. Yet, like the previous recessions, the financial repercussions were still very limited. The number of banks that failed was small—seven—and dominated by those that were adversely affected by bad checks or embezzlement. These included the First State Bank of Bonne Terre, Missouri; the Eatontown National Bank of New Jersey; the Farmers Bank of Petersburg, Kentucky; the Peoples State Savings Bank of Auburn, Michigan; and the State Bank of Prairie City, Iowa. These five institutions ranged in size from just $1.2 million in deposits to $15.9 million. The other two banks to fail did so as the result of unsound lending practices—essentially loans were made in excess of lending limits, and large loans were made to unsecured borrowers. The largest of these was the City Bank of Philadelphia, with $8.8 million in assets, while the Berea Bank and Trust Company in Kentucky had $5.5 billion in deposits. This was only the second recession in the postwar period in which banks failed because of their lending practices. The Peoples State Bank of Richland, Texas, was the first to fail during a postwar recession (1957–1958) as a result of bad loans.

The limited number of bank failures during this recession is a bit surprising, given that the Fed used Regulation Q to set interest rate ceilings on time deposits, in 1966, as a means to restrict the banking system's ability to extend credit. The resulting contraction in credit became known as the credit crunch of 1966.

Although the recession caused only a limited dislocation in the financial sector, the real economy took a big hit with the bankruptcy of Penn Central Railroad, in the face of a huge cash squeeze, caused by heavy losses in both its passenger and freight operations. The bankruptcy would be the largest in the postwar period, to that point, as the railroad was the sixth largest public company at the start of the year. The bankruptcy affected 94,000 employees, and required an immediate government-guaranteed loan of $200 million to keep the railroad in operation, as its businesses were considered vital by the Department of Transportation. Penn Central had reported a $121.6 million loss in 1969, and had already lost $80 million through the second quarter of 1970. This dismal performance caused investors to balk at a $100 million debt offering, in May 1970,which was set to pay more than 10 percent to investors.

Federal Deposit Insurance Corporation Failures and Assistance Transactions (Dollar Amounts in Thousands) 1969–1970 Recession

Institution Name	Location	Effective Date	Ins. Fund	Transaction Type	Failure / Assistance	Total Deposits	Total Assets
Berea Bank and Trust Company	Berea, KY	10/8/70	FDIC	P&A	FAILURE	5,375	5,871
City Bank of Philadelphia	Philadelphia, PA	9/3/70	FDIC	P&A	FAILURE	8,839	10,775
First State Bank of Bonne Terre	Bonne Terre, MO	8/24/70	FDIC	P&A	FAILURE	7,118	8,003
Eatontown National Bank	Eatontown, NJ	8/7/70	FDIC	PO	FAILURE	15,912	21,417
Farmers Bank of Petersburg	Petersburg, KY	6/25/70	FDIC	PO	FAILURE	1,259	1,074
The Peoples State Savings Bank	Auburn, MI	4/18/70	FDIC	PO	FAILURE	9,940	10,877
State Bank of Prairie City	Prairie City, IA	2/22/70	FDIC	PO	FAILURE	3,897	4,130

Source: FDIC HSOB Bank & Thrift Failures, December 1969–November 1970

The second phase of postwar business cycles was also caused by policies designed to contain (rein in) inflation. The three cycles experienced between 1973 and 1982 were dominated by supply-side constraints, in contrast to the excess aggregate demand that led to the previous five recessions. A combination of repeated energy shocks and an aggressive program of credit controls caused the next series of downturns in the economy. Politics and energy prices commingled to cause the November 1973 to March 1975 oil crisis recession.

The official reason given for the quadrupling of oil prices was OPEC's unhappiness with US arms sales to Israel, to replenish weapons depleted in the Yom Kippur War with Egypt and Syria. The oil embargo sent prices spiraling upward and caused supply shortages and long lines at gas stations across the country. The economic reason behind the embargo and the associated spike in prices was the fact that the dollar had been declining in value, and OPEC's purchasing power was being reduced dramatically—especially because US companies were also raising prices for everything from agricultural goods to heavy construction equipment, as the dollar declined.

The six-month January to July 1980 recession, on the other hand, was the result of credit controls undertaken by the Fed, at the insistence of the Carter administration. The speed at which these controls pushed the economy into recession led to their quick reversal. As a result, the economy entered a period of stagflation—a period of below-trend growth, stagnant labor market, and accelerating inflation. Aggregate demand reacted to the reversal in credit constraints more quickly than did the supply side of the economy, and when combined with a second oil embargo in the wake of the Iranian Revolution, led to a second recession (July 1981 to November 1982) in just two years, and the establishment of a wage-price spiral. This labor market dynamic resulted in a dangerous new economic development—stagflation, which subsequently led to a pronounced shift in the thrust of monetary policy.

Instead of monetary policy supporting fiscal policy decisions, the Fed, under Paul Volcker, limited the effect of the

Reagan supply-side revolution by hiking rates, inverting the yield curve for an extended period, and driving up the exchange value of the dollar. This fundamental change in the policy mix confronting the economy would eventually lead to a shift in the nature of the business cycle, from inflation cycles to credit cycles. Early signs of this change in cycle dynamics surfaced late in the 1973 to 1982 supply-induced inflation cycles. One obvious indication that the economy and markets had begun to evolve is evident in the number of financial institutions that failed in the wake of a recession, and the size of the institution involved. The 1973–1975 recession resulted in twenty-three bank failures, the largest of which was Franklin National Bank of New York with $1.4 million in deposits and $3.7 million in assets.

Twenty-two additional banks failed during the six-month January to July 1980 recession. The largest bank to fail during the Carter credit crunch–induced recession was First Pennsylvania Bank of Philadelphia with $5 million in deposits and just under $8 million in assets, at the time it failed. Bank failures spiked to 159 during the Reagan recession, which stretched from July 1981 to November 1982. Although the size of failed institutions was relatively small, compared to Franklin National and First Pennsylvania, the magnitude of the effect on the industry was huge, totaling almost $45 billion in deposits, and $57.5 billion in assets. This evolution from isolated bank failures to bigger and more broad-based failures reflects the growing dependence on debt financing, and the transition in the economy from one of aggregate demand leading business cycles to one of supply constraints causing inflation. Monetary and fiscal policies were well suited to deal with excess demand situations, but not with inflation induced by a supply shock. The result was a series of financial accidents associated with each of the next three business cycles, which were increasingly complex in nature, and involved larger financial institutions that were more complicated to resolve.

Supply constraints proved to be a drag on underlying growth and resulted in rising interest rates at both ends of the yield curve. Lower trend growth and higher interest rates left companies searching for ways to boost their top-line revenue, and increased leverage was an easy way to reverse the growing malaise. This increased dependence on debt-related financing increased the role of credit in deterring how the business cycle evolved. In fact, the last three business cycles of the postwar period were credit induced, not inflation induced. The July 1990 to March 1991 recession resulted from the collapse of the thrift industry, while the March 2001 to November 2001 recession was caused by corporate malfeasance, which led to a forced restructuring of corporate balance sheets. The latest postwar cycle—the long and deep December 2007–June 2009 cycle—was the result of the housing bubble burst that crushed household balance sheets, and pulled the banking industry down with it.

The evolution of financial dislocations from one-off failures of small institutions, principally the result of fraud or mismanagement, to larger systemically important failures will be analyzed, and then we will review the credit dislocation

that caused the last three business cycles. These larger systemically important institutions failed as a result of the pressure
on management to produce strong earnings, and show growth
in a rapidly changing financial market environment. This evolution also increased the international nature of these disruptions. As such, the size of these failures increased, as did the
difficulty for policymakers to resolve them.

Chapter 13

From Small to Large and Systemically Important

The postwar period is littered with financial institutions, principally banks, that either failed as a result of the business cycle or, more recently, caused the economic contraction. There was a difference between bank failures during the postwar period and those that occurred prior to World War II, because institutions and regulations were put in place to avoid a repeat of the Great Depression. For a time, the financial dislocations that haunted the banking industry in the postwar period were small, and one-off events, typically resulting from fraud or mismanagement. However, as the economy evolved and financial markets and banking became increasingly international and interconnected, recession-induced dislocations became larger, and more difficult to resolve. In this chapter, three bank failures will be reviewed, one associated with each of the three business cycles of the period from 1973 to 1982. Each of these failures reveals important new aspects of bank failures, and sets the stage for an important shift in the nature of business cycles. Rather than business cycles causing financial disruptions, credit cycles (financial dislocations) led the business cycle.

The first recession of this period, the 1973–1975 oil crisis recession, led to the failure of Franklin National Bank of New York. Franklin National was once the twentieth largest bank in the United States. From its start as a retail bank in Long Island, Franklin was an innovator in offering new products and services to grow its business. In 1947, Franklin introduced junior savings accounts, and in 1950, the drive-up teller window. The bank's credit card was introduced in 1951 to help local merchants compete with larger chain department stores. The bank installed outdoor teller machines in 1968, and pioneered Franklin Savings bonds that later developed into certificates of deposit (CDs), in 1969. As a result, the bank expanded rapidly in the 1960s and '70s. After New York State passed a law in 1960 allowing banks to operate in multiple counties, Franklin opened a branch in New York City, to fend off competition from powerful city banks that quickly moved into Franklin's backyard of Nassau and Suffolk counties.

The transformation from domestic to international banking was largely the result of US banking laws that limited the geographic spread of banks as a means of keeping a problem in one region from spreading to other areas of the country. This post-Depression limitation increased the attractiveness of growth-oriented banks to expand overseas. Moreover, there were no reserve requirements on overseas deposits, nor were there limits on the size of overseas lending, such as making domestic loans relative to capital. As a result, US banks were incentivized to expand, and become multinational corporations. In 1965, 13 US banks had 211 overseas branches. By 1975, 126 American banks had 762 overseas branches. US banks had $9.1 billion in assets in their overseas branches in 1965, and $145.3 billion ten years later. These overseas businesses became a vital source of earnings. By 1970, earnings from overseas accounted for 25 percent of total earnings of the twelve major money center banks. This share grew to half of their earnings, by 1975.

Dramatic growth resulted in international financial markets, especially the Eurocurrency and foreign exchange markets. The interbank (LIBOR market) grew to more than $380 billion in 1977, from just $14 billion in 1956. With the advent of floating exchange rates in 1971, when the Nixon administration ended gold convertibility, the volume of foreign exchange transitions ballooned. For example, in 1974 alone, the twelve major US multinational banks bought and sold some $33 billion in the foreign exchange markets.

The competition in wholesale banking in New York City was tough, and Franklin was forced to pay up to attract deposits, principally brokered deposits. The bank needed to make loans that other banks shied away from, in order to accumulate assets. As pressure on earnings grew, Franklin joined the movement abroad. It established branches in Nassau, Bahamas, and in London, where it became heavily involved in Eurodollar markets and in foreign exchange. The bank even attracted a foreign owner, an Italian financier, who was reputedly tied to the Mafia, the Vatican Bank, and the Nixon administration. By 1973, Franklin had assets of more than $5 billion; it also had several significant problems: weak management, a bad domestic loan portfolio, poor investment portfolio, and a heavy reliance on short-term deposits backing long-term loans. In May 1974, Franklin failed, becoming part of the first international banking crisis.

Size of Eurocurrency Market and of Interbank Portion of Eurocurrency Market ($ Billion)

Size	1970	1971	1972	1973	1974	1975	1976	1977
Gross size including inter-Eurobank transactions	111	145	200	303	370	457	559	660
Net size	65	85	110	160	215	250	310	380
Inter-Eurobank market	46	60	90	143	155	207	249	280
Inter-Eurobank market as percentage of gross size	41%	41%	45%	47%	42%	45%	45%	42%

Source: Morgan Guaranty Trust Company, World Financial Markets (March 1978), The Failure of the Franklin National Bank, Joan E. Spero

On October 8, 1974, after five months of persistent crisis, Franklin National Bank was declared insolvent. The bank's failure can be credited to a host of problems, both domestic and international, in nature, as well as poor management, and of course, fraud. But it is the international aspect that makes the failure of Franklin so important, regarding the November 1973 to March 1975 recession.

Franklin's domestic problems were the result of rapid growth and poor management that left the bank heavily dependent on short-term borrowing to fund longer-term loans. Franklin's dependence on short-term funding was evident in the growth of its borrowing in the market for federal funds. Specifically, in 1964, federal funds and repurchase agreements accounted for 5 percent of the bank's outstanding liabilities, but accounted for 11 percent by 1972. Its dependence on certificates of deposit was also said to have been substantial, representing about 13 percent of its liabilities, in 1974. At the same time, the bank's domestic demand, time, and savings deposit bases declined from 83.5 percent in 1964, to 51.6 percent in 1974. The bank's capital, as a source of funds, also declined during this period, from 8.1 percent of resources in 1964, to only 4 percent in 1973.

Reliance on short-term funding contributed significantly to the bank's disappointing earnings, and thus its push overseas. Not only were such funds more expansive than traditional deposits, they were also highly interest-rate sensitive. The rise or fall in market rates was quickly reflected in Franklin's cost of funds, while its interest income remained more stable. As the problems at Franklin mounted, concerns about its credit worthiness forced it to pay a premium to borrow, adding to its operating costs, and squeezing its margins.

Another expense adding to Franklin's problems was rising loan losses. As the bank expanded into New York City, its eagerness to grow caused it to take on loans that other banks were unwilling to make. Franklin's questionable lending practices were very visible, as in May 1974, when 58.7 percent of its loans were listed as classified, or criticized by bank examiners, representing 62 percent of bank capital; loan losses totaled $13.4 million that year. The bank was also saddled with low income on its loans and investments—another key domestic problem. Franklin was heavily invested in low yielding tax-free municipal bonds that accounted for 60 percent of its overall securities investments. These investments made sense when the bank had taxable income, but as profits declined and rates rose, these investments further dragged down profitability.

It is also evident that Franklin was improperly positioned for rising rates as Net Income as a percent of Total Operating Income was being squeezed. By the 1970s, Franklin was caught in a profit squeeze. Its interest rate spread declined to just 1 percent in 1973, from 2.6 percent in 1971, and it went negative at one point in 1974.

The international side of Franklin National Bank's failure was most apparent in its heavy losses in foreign exchange trading. Management's push overseas, and into speculative trading, was motivated by a desire to offset losses in other divisions, and ironically, this move pushed the bank into failure. In the

Franklin New York Corporation Net Income as Percentage of Total Operating Income

1964	11.5%
1965	8.7
1966	5.5
1967	8.9
1968	10.3
1969	11.0
1970	9.9
1971	8.8
1972	6.6
1973	3.7

Source: The Failure of the Franklin National Bank, Joan E. Spero

period of fixed exchange rates, banks typically engaged in foreign exchange trading, primarily for their own needs, or those of their customers. The era of floating exchange rates and wider fluctuations caused Franklin's growth-oriented management to speculate in the currency markets, to add to profitability.

The bank's relationship with the Italian financier Michele Sindona was also instrumental in this push into foreign exchange trading, and facilitated many illegal transactions made by Franklin's employees to hide losses resulting from its currency trading division. To help hide these losses, the bank also rapidly expanded its currency trading until other banks began to question the scope of its operations, and subsequently informed the Federal Reserve that they would no longer do business with Franklin. Following a series of meetings with

Franklin's management, and investigations into its foreign exchange dealings, the Federal Reserve established a task force to review Franklin's performance on a weekly basis, and made contingency plans to allow Franklin's access to the discount window, if necessary. The situation erupted into a crisis in early May after the Federal Reserve Board of Governors denied Franklin's request to acquire Talcott National Corporation, owned by Sindona. The official reason for the denial was that the merger would place excessive demands on Franklin's weak internal structure, but many in the markets saw it as concern over Sindona's influence on the domestic financial system.

Just two days later, Franklin's clearing bank in London objected to the size of Franklin's trading in sterling, and an inquiry revealed unauthorized and hidden transactions in several currencies, and the possibility of significant losses. Franklin's borrowing in the market for reserves traded between banks also began to dry up. This was quickly followed by declines in the price of Franklin's common and preferred shares. The Securities and Exchange Commission reacted to the growing problem at Franklin by insisting that it suspend its dividend, and immediately after, trading in Franklin was stopped, on the exchange. These steps destroyed the markets' confidence in the bank, and on May 13, 1974, the bank experienced a crippling run on its deposits. But foreign exchange trading losses were not its only international problem—a bigger issue was its Eurodollar dealings.

Unlike most of its lending, Franklin's euro lending book was high in quality, with a healthy mix of fixed-rate and adjustable-rate loans. Where the bank ran into trouble was its entry into the market, late in the game, when spreads had already shrunk to just .375–.50 of a percent. Moreover, because interest rates on these loans rose only twice a year, the bank's funding costs were driven by market movements, and sudden, sharp swings in rates could eliminate any spread in their lending. In fact, as rates soared in 1973–1974, Franklin found itself paying more for its funding than it was earning on its Eurodollar loan book. As its currency market difficulties surfaced, Franklin's problems worsened, with banks charging a premium in the LIBOR market, for its funding. It is estimated that by mid-1974, Franklin's London branch had accumulated losses of $1.2 million on its Eurodollar lending. By October 6, 1974, the bank was declared insolvent, and exposed the risks that an unregulated international banking market could impose on the domestic banking systems.

The Carter credit crunch recession that lasted only from January to July 1980, resulted in the failure of First Pennsylvania Bank N.A. that March. Whereas Franklin National's failure was the first of the postwar period to expose the risks involved with international banking, First Pennsylvania's failure became the first federal bailout of a national bank, as it was the only course of action regulators could take that would not undermine confidence in the financial system. This potential undermining of a financial system is known as **systemic risk**. Aggressive and risky lending and investing had turned First Pennsylvania into Philadelphia's largest bank, but huge losses and panicked depositors led to an unprecedented $500 million government bailout.

The bank's problem has been described as the classic "goof"—putting too many eggs in one basket. Essentially, the bank's management bet the wrong way on interest rates by investing too heavily in long-term government bonds. This bet on the direction of rates pulled the bank down. Rising, instead of falling, interest rates caused the value of the bank's bond portfolio to decline, and with it, the bank's earnings. Its rush to speculate in bonds was driven by a deteriorating loan portfolio, especially in real estate. First Pennsylvania had become heavily involved in real estate investment trusts, whose value began to decline in 1974, and by 1976 the bank's percentage of nonperforming loans was more than triple that of the average of the top fifteen banks, and 50 percent worse than the weakest of the top group. These loan losses, and a lack of reserve provisioning by management to maintain its dividend, left the bank in search of a new revenue stream, and exposed to further losses. The bank also had larger deposits than most banks its size, and all were fully insured. As such, when it failed in 1980, it received open bank assistance from the FDIC, making it the first national bank to be bailed out by the government.

First Pennsylvania was the successor of the first domestic private bank, and it had assets of $8 billion, and deposits of $5.3 billion, spread across 574,000 accounts. The bank operated sixty-nine offices, including forty branches in Philadelphia, as well as others operating in the US Virgin Islands, London, and Nassau, Bahamas. In the late 1960s and early 1970s, First Pennsylvania grew rapidly. Assets increased to $8 billion from $2.1 billion at its peak. These were largely

Non-Performing Assets, 1976 (in Millions of Dollars)

	OREO	Non-Accrual Loans	Re-Negotiated Loans	Total Non-Performing Loans	% of Non-Performing Loans per Category	% of all Non-Performing Loans	Total Loans per Category	% of Non-Per-forming Loans to All Loans
First Pennsylvania								
REITS	N/A	11.9	68.7	80.6	81	N/A	99	2.1
Non-Bank Financial Institutions	N/A	5.6	10.0	15.6	5.3	N/A	292	NEG
Real Estate Construction, Development	N/A	128.8	42.1	170.9	61.5	N/A	278	4.4
Real Estate Commercial, Permanent	N/A	44.4	N/A	44.4	20.0	N/A	222	1.1
Total, Four Categories	73	190.7	120.8	384.5	39.9	63	964	10.0
Commercial, Industrial	N/A	90.1	112.0	202.1	13.7	N/A	1,474	5.2
Total	73	299.0	239.0	611.0	100.0	N/A	3,861	15.8
BankAmerica	35	289	262.0	586	N/A	N/A	35,448	1.7
Chase Manhattan	280	1,386	325.0	1,991	N/A	N/A	30,663	6.5
Bankers Trust NY	118	569	413.0	1,100	N/A	N/A	11,347	9.7
First Chicago	96	976	152.0	1,224	N/A	N/A	11,720	10.4
Manufacturers Hanover Trust	91	295	202	588	N/A	N/A	17,610	3.3
							Average of Top 15: 5.1	

Source: Annual Reports and Loeb, Rhoades, ERI News Service Special Report, Volume 4, Number 22

real estate loans, many of which went bad as the housing market slumped, in the wake of rising interest rates. The Federal Reserve increased its discount rate to 11.8 percent in 1980, and mortgage rates rose to 13.8 percent. This backup in rates was a reaction to OPEC's oil embargo, and caused both deposit and loan rates to rise.

Beginning in 1976, First Pennsylvania had started to use short-term deposit liabilities to make large bets in long-term government bonds, to offset losses accumulating in its loan portfolio. As interest rates rose, the interest margin was squeezed, and eventually turned into negative carry. The bank had accumulated a portfolio of 10-year notes and 30-year bonds, paying between 7.6 percent and 7.9 percent per year, while its deposit rates rose to a high of 15.5 percent, in 1980. Its bond portfolio is estimated to have lost the bank $300 million. Additionally, at the end of the first quarter of 1980, a very high 6.3 percent of the bank's loan assets were not paying any interest, adding to its losses. As a result, short-term depositors began to trim their balances, and the bank suffered a liquidity squeeze. The bank could not sell its securities portfolio because it would have had to realize a sizable hit from its depreciated value. The result was FDIC intervention, but with no suitable purchaser available in the state, and the FDIC's own insurance fund only $9.6 billion, at the time, paying off the deposits and closing the bank was possibly seen as *undermining confidence in the safety of the financial system.* This left a public bailout as the only course of action. The terms of the package agreed to include $1.5 billion in total assistance.

Terms of the assistance program for First Pennsylvania Bank N.A., under the FDIC's open bank assistance authority, included in the Federal Deposit Act of 1950:

- The FDIC would provide a five-year subordinated note for $350 million, which was interest free for the first year, and would be 8.50 percent for the remaining four years. The FDIC's note would be senior to all other subordinated debt, other than that provided by other banks.

- A group of twenty-seven leading banks would provide a $175 million subordinated note at an interest rate equal to Citibank's one-year CD rate, adjusted annually.

- The Federal Reserve provided a $1 billion line of credit through its discount window.

- With the increase in its liquidity, First Pennsylvania was required to sell a portion of its Treasury portfolio, incurring a loss of up to $75 million.

- The package would include $20 million in warrants in the holding company's stock being provided to the FDIC ($13 million) and the twenty-seven participating banks ($7 million). These warrants would be good for seven years, and any proceeds exercised from the warrants had to be invested in the bank's capital account.

The first two recessions of the period from 1975 to 1982 saw the size of bank failures associated with the downturn increase substantially. In fact, First Pennsylvania was the largest to date to fail, and had to be bailed out at a time when thrift institutions were being allowed to fail, and equity holders were being forced to absorb significant losses. The failure of Franklin National also highlighted the risks associated with the largely unregulated international banking market, and how events in one country could influence banks and markets in other countries. The third and deepest recession of this nine-year period revealed the risk of contagion—how the failure of one bank could lead to the failure of other equally important institutions. These three important developments in the nature of bank failures highlight how credit cycles have evolved from banking system disintermediation, to exposed fraud, to industry and systemic failure in the period from 1990 to the present. Moreover, it can be argued that credit cycles now lead business cycles.

· · ·

The collapse of Penn Square Bank N.A. in Oklahoma City coincided with the 1980s oil glut, and it proved to be the first of 139 Oklahoma banks to fail during the decade. Not only did other banks in Oklahoma fail as a result of oil lending that soured as the price of crude tumbled, but Penn Square's failure triggered the failure of important institutions from one side of the country to the other. For instance, losses at Seattle First National Bank were traced back to Penn Square. The FDIC forced Seattle First to merge with Bank of America, due to these losses. The failure of Continental Illinois Bank and Trust can also be traced back to its relationship with Penn Square. This domino effect became known as contagion, and it has become an important financial risk ever since.

Penn Square became the first bank, since the FDIC was formed, in which uninsured depositors suffered losses, as no other bank was willing to assume its deposits. Penn Square failed on July 5, 1982, about halfway through the July 1981 to November 1982 recession precipitated by the Iranian energy crisis. The bank failed with $470.4 million in deposits, and $516.8 million in assets, after growing from $62 million in assets in 1977 to $520 million by mid-1982. Penn Square grew by making large and speculative loans, primarily to oil and gas companies, and selling interest in these loans in the form of participation loans—a new and innovative product—while retaining servicing of the loans. At the time it failed, Penn Square was servicing about $2 billion in loans it had originated, but no longer owned.

From the beginning, Penn Square failed to document its loans properly, and it based repayment on collateral value, rather than the borrower's ability to pay the loan. Documentation of collateral was also deficient, a problem that would complicate the bank's resolution. To avoid limits on the amount of credit extended to any one borrower, Penn Square made aggressive use of selling participation loans to other banks. Its initial loan participation sales were made to Continental Illinois National Bank and Trust Company. As oil prices spiked with the overthrow of the Shah of Iran in 1979, Penn Square began selling participations to other large banks, including Seattle First National Bank, Northern Trust Company of Chicago, Chase Manhattan Bank of New York, and Michigan National Bank of Lansing, all of which wanted to get involved in oil lending, as prices of the commodity rose, but were geographically constrained.

The Office of the Comptroller of the Currency was concerned about the concentration of oil and gas lending by Penn Square, as early as 1977. Subsequent examinations highlighted low capital, low loan quality, inexperienced staff, increasing loan losses, and a low level of loan loss reserves. When oil prices peaked in 1981 at $36.95 per barrel, and then began to fall sharply, the problems at Penn Square began to attract the attention of participating banks. By April, an examination of the bank by regulators suggested that the bank raise an additional $7 million in capital, and take a $10 million charge against its loan book. Just a month later, concerns among depositors caused the bank to rely increasingly on brokered deposits, and by June 1982, it was apparent that Penn Square was about to fail.

The fact that more than 50 percent of Penn Square's deposits were uninsured caused regulators to worry that paying off only the insured depositors would have adverse consequences for the stability of the banking system. Typically, uninsured deposits accounted for less than 5 percent of total deposits. Among the uninsured were twenty-nine commercial banks, forty-four savings and loans, and 221 credit unions. However,

The Last Twelve Bank Payoffs Before Penn Square ($ in Millions)

Bank Name and Location	Total Deposits	Date
Watkins Banking Company, Faunsdale, Alabama	1.7	07/24/78
Village Bank, Pueblo West, Colorado	5.0	01/26/79
Bank of Enville, Enville, Tennessee	3.5	06/16/79
The Farmers State Bank, Protection, Kansas	5.0	09/21/79
Bank of Lake Helen, Lake Helen, Florida	4.2	01/11/80
First National Bank of Carrington, Carrington, North Dakota	11.5	02/12/80
The Citizens State Bank, Viola, Kansas	1.9	06/04/80
The Des Plaines Bank, Des Plaines, Illinois	46.3	03/14/81
Southwestern Bank, Tucson, Arizona	4.7	09/25/81
The Bank of Woodson, Woodson, Texas	3.2	03/01/82
Carroll County Bank, Huntingdon, Tennessee	8.2	04/30/82
Citizens Bank, Tillar, Arkansas	6.7	06/23/82
Penn Square N.A., Oklahoma	207.5	07/05/82

Source: FDIC, Historical Statistics on Banking: A Statistical History of the United States Banking Industry, 1934–1992, Pages 615–618, Managing the Crisis, Page 520

the size of Penn Square's contingent liabilities, some $2.1 billion in participations, kept the FDIC from merging Penn Square with another bank. The FDIC realized that it would have been required to protect the acquiring institution from losses on these obligations, in addition to paying off all uninsured depositors. In receivership, the uninsured deposits were lumped in with the general creditors. These depositors were given receivership certificates, and to help with potential liquidity problems, the Federal Reserve allowed holders of these certificates to borrow up to 90 percent of the discounted value of these certificates. The discount amounted to approximately 70.4 percent of the face value. Penn Square proved to be the largest bank payout by the FDIC in its history, to that time. The bank's poor lending practices weakened the financial condition of other larger banks, spreading its problems to other banks across the country.

Chapter 14

From One-Off to Industry and Sector-Wide Dislocations

A transition in the nature of bank failures and credit-related events associated with recessions began to surface in the early 1970s, and has continued to evolve over the final three recessions of the postwar period. Business cycles have generally been caused by the Federal Reserve's desire to control inflation, over the past seventy years. The Regulation Q liquidity crisis of the mid-1960s and the Carter credit controls that resulted in the 1980 recession are two exceptions that need to be identified, in the interest of being complete. As such, financial dislocations have tended to be a side effect of recessions, rather than lead them.

The shift to credit cycles (financial dislocations) that drive the business cycle began to take shape with the Penn Square Bank N.A. of Oklahoma debacle. The failure of Penn Square had a domino effect, causing bank failures stretching from Seattle to Chicago. The role of contagion became even more evident in the 1990s, with the savings and loan crisis, and again in the 2001 recession with accounting irregularities that led to the demise of several previously high-flying, nonfinancial corporate entities. The financial crisis of 2007 may have caught policymakers, and the banking industry, by surprise, but the history presented so far suggests it was the natural progression of credit cycles in a world dominated by excess supply, rather than excess demand. Contagion risk and credit cycles are likely to be the new norm rather than the exception.

The three business cycles experienced since 1990 have each been unique in many ways, but most important, all three have been associated with and, to an extent, caused by credit problems that have accumulated during their expansion phase. In fact, the rate of inflation—the consumer price index (CPI) excluding food and energy—peaked at 13.6 percent in June 1980, and has been on a downtrend ever since. The anti-inflation policies advanced by the Volcker Fed, and the supply-side policies promoted by President Ronald Reagan, began a long transition in the economy from excess demand to excess supply. The result has been a clear downtrend in inflation and a significant reduction in inflation volatility, especially during the current expansion. Excess supply, however, cannot eliminate all cyclical inflation pressures; as such, the Fed and the market's collective memory of the late-1970s wage-price spiral have kept the Federal Open Market Committee's anti-inflation policies an important determinant in every business cycle.

The history of inflation over the past three business cycles is one of successively lower bottoms being achieved after each cyclical trough—with the headline inflation rate dipping into negative territory for eight consecutive months in 2008. This was the first time since an eleven-month decline in 1949–1950, that the headline CPI was negative for an extended period. Despite this downtrend, the Fed's response to a cyclical rise in inflation has become more preemptive, and each response has triggered a different credit event that dominated the recession, and dictated the nature of the recovery.

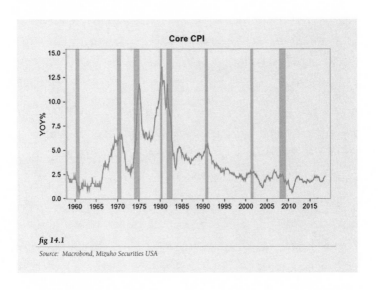

fig 14.1

Source: *Macrobond, Mizuho Securities USA*

The July 1990 to March 1991 recession has been credited to the Gulf War, and the spike in energy prices that followed on the heels of Iraq's invasion of Kuwait. The passage of the North American Free Trade Agreement exacerbated the downturn, as companies had been in the process of moving production facilities to Mexico to reduce costs, and higher energy prices accelerated this process. The failed leveraged buyout of United Airlines by its unions added to the economy's problems as it triggered an overdue equity market correction, further squeezing credit availability, all while the economy was reeling from the demise of the thrift industry. Although the savings and loan crisis had been brewing for years, it exploded in the run-up to the ninth postwar recession, and led to an atypically sluggish recovery. The tenth recession of the postwar period has been credited to the collapse of the Dot-Com Bubble and the September 11 attacks. More important, the accounting scandals that led to the failure of several large nonfinancial companies forced a restructuring of the corporate sector's balance sheet. This focus on repairing balance sheets led companies to pull back on investment spending, which had powered the expansion and had been perceived to be a virtuous cycle of capital spending, and rising household wealth, boosting the expansion.

Whereas the thrift industry failure contributed to the 1990 recession, balance sheet restructuring across the entire nonfinancial corporate sector was the key factor behind the March to November 2001 recession. Credit-related distortions played an even larger role in the most recent business cycle, which stretched from December 2007 to June 2009. A collapse in home prices began in 2005 as the Federal Reserve hiked rates, leaving households too heavily leveraged in real estate in a declining market, forcing banks to pull back credit availability, and thus triggering a recession. The downturn in housing forced both the household sector and the banking industry to restructure, at the same time. This was the first time since the Great Depression that multiple balance sheets within the economy had to be repaired simultaneously. The result was an abnormally deep recession, and a drawn-out recovery phase. The trough was established only after monetary policy was pushed beyond traditional limits into new and innovative schemes, to stem the collapse in liquidity, and to get ahead of the curve. We will discuss this continued evolution of the role of credit/financial dislocations in business cycles in further detail, beginning with the thrift industry's role in the 1990 downturn.

The savings and loan crisis, as it came to be called, was a broad banking industry problem that lasted from 1986 to 1989, but its roots stretched back to 1979. In an effort to break the back of an inflationary spiral that had gripped the economy after the oil crisis of the mid-1970s, the Federal Reserve began a tightening cycle in 1979 that would double the interest rate it charged its member banks. This sudden increase in funding costs hit the savings and loan industry hard. Savings and loans made long-term, fixed-rate mortgages that were funded with short-term deposits, and with Regulation Q limiting what banks paid depositors, they could not attract adequate capital, and became insolvent. Regulators quickly realized that the insurance fund they had set up to deal with savings and loans' failures was inadequate, and they began to relax regulations on these institutions in the hope that they could grow out of their problem. As it turned out, this effort to rescue savings and loans through deregulation, a policy championed by the Reagan White House, increased competition not only among these institutions, but also from commercial banks. This adverse situation subsequently led to inappropriate lending decisions, and an overbuilding in multiple real estate markets. Eventually, a collapse in commercial real estate prices triggered a simultaneous correction in the commercial banking industry, and a collapse in the thrift industry. The decision by regulators to let the industry grow out of its problems greatly increased their scope and the eventual cost of dealing with both problems that surfaced in the commercial banking industry, and the large number of thrifts that failed.

Inflation of the late 1970s and early 1980s resulted from accommodative monetary policy and the simultaneous fiscal policy stimulus, provided by the Johnson Great Society experiment, and military expenses required for fighting the Vietnam War. The October 1979 shift in monetary policy orchestrated by then–Fed Chairman Volcker rattled financial markets and altered the financial market environment so abruptly that it weakened the foundation of the thrift industry. In fact, 118 savings and loans failed, from 1980 to 1982, costing the Federal Savings and Loan Insurance Company (FSLIC) an estimated $3.5 billion. This deterioration in the industry was unprecedented, and it left the insurance fund with little in the way of resources to deal with further problems. By the end of 1982, an estimated 415 savings and loans were still technically insolvent, and the cost to resolve these institutions would be an additional $25 billion. The FSLIC had only $6.3 billion in reserves at the time, and the political will to address these problems head-on was nonexistent.

Selected Statistics, FSLIC-Insured Savings and Loans, 1980–1989 ($ Billions)

Year	Number of S&Ls	Total Assets	Net Income	Tangible Capital	Tangible Capital/ Total Assets	No. Insolvent S&Ls	Assets in Insolvent S&Ls	FSLIC Reserves
1980	3,993	$604	$0.8	$32	5.3%	43	$0.4	$6.5
1981	3,751	640	-4.6	25	4.0	112	28.5	6.2
1982	3,287	686	-4.1	4	0.5	415	220.0	6.3
1983	3,146	814	1.9	4	0.4	515	284.6	6.4
1984	3,136	976	1.0	3	0.3	695	360.2	5.6
1985	3,246	1,068	3.7	8	0.8	705	358.3	4.6
1986	3,220	1,162	0.1	14	1.2	672	343.1	-6.3
1987	3,147	1,249	-7.8	9	0.7	672	353.8	-13.7
1988	2,949	1,349	-13.4	22	1.6	508	297.3	-75.0
1989	2,878	1,252	-17.6	10	0.8	516	290.8	NA

Source: An Examination of the Banking Crises of the 1980s and Early 1990s

The lack of political will to deal with the problems, and the fact that the savings and loan industry accounted for approximately 50 percent of the home loan market, at the time, forced regulators into forbearance—i.e., allowing insolvent institutions to stay in business in the hope that they could grow out of their problems. To help the industry, Congress passed several important pieces of legislation: the Depository Institution Deregulation and Monetary Control Act of 1980, and the Garn-St Germain Depository Institutions Act of 1982. These legislative efforts significantly expanded the thrift industry's lending authority, and reduced its regulatory oversight.

Essentially, savings and loans were now able to compete more directly with commercial banks, but without FDIC regulatory oversight. The new rules also authorized the use of more lenient accounting rules to report their financial conditions, and eliminated the restrictions on the minimum number of shareholders. This substantially eased a key barrier for entry into the industry, resulting in significant increases in de novo institutions. Many of these new institutions would subsequently fail because they were thinly capitalized, and tended to invest in increasingly riskier assets to earn a competitive return in an era of high funding costs. These institutions also tended to rely on brokered deposits that proved to be more costly and sensitive to an institution's financial conditions, but did facilitate rapid growth. The effect of these changes allowed thrift assets to grow by 56 percent between 1982 and 1985, while commercial banks grew by only 24 percent over this same period.

Number of Newly Chartered FSLIC-Insured S&Ls, 1980–1986

Year	State-Chartered	Federally Chartered	Total
1980	63	5	68
1981	21	4	25
1982	23	3	26
1983	36	11	47
1984	68	65	133
1985	45	43	88
1986	13	14	27
TOTAL	348	144	492

Source: An Examination of the Banking Crises of the 1980s and Early 1990s

A combination of the Federal Reserve's war on inflation and lack of political will to deal with the savings and loan crisis early in its formation was complemented by the Reagan administration's belief that deregulation was the key to all economic problems. This led to much bigger problems in the late 1980s and early 1990s, and contributed to back-to-back recessions, and the first jobless recovery of the postwar period. Regulatory forbearance, imprudent and risky lending, as well as brokered deposits, all contributed to the demise of the thrift industry. Between 1986 and 1995, the FSLIC closed or resolved through merger, 296 institutions, and the government's bailout of the industry through the Resolution Trust Corporation resolved an additional 747 institutions between 1989 and 1995, at an estimated cost of $160 billion. This was well beyond the $45 billion initial estimate to clean up the problem, back in 1982.

Efforts to help the savings and loan industry grow out if its problems put thrifts into direct competition with commercial banks at a time when the Reagan administration had passed the Economic Recovery Tax Act (ERTA), which provided a significant incentive for real estate development projects. ERTA allowed for accelerated depreciation, which, when combined with real estate limited partnerships and the ability to use passive depreciation losses against active income, to lower taxable income, stimulated a rapid expansion in new real estate investments. The rush to grow by thrifts, and to exploit their new competitiveness, contributed to an explosion in nonresidential and residential commercial investment spending, supported by commercial banks and thrifts. As such, commercial spending as a share of GDP increased from just 1.3 percent in 1979, to 2 percent by 1985, with the level of spending on such projects more than doubling, to $84.1 billion. This expansion outstripped demand, and by 1986 the office vacancy rate had increased to 16.5 percent, up from just 5.2 percent in 1979. Multifamily building permits also increased by almost 50 percent over this boom period. By 1986 it became clear that ERTA had provided too much of an incentive for real estate investment, and that overbuilding was becoming an economic problem. Congress, as a result, passed the Tax Reform Act of 1986 that, among other things, eliminated the ability for taxpayers to offset ordinary income with passive losses. This resulted in a booming real estate building turning into a bust. Along with a downturn in new construction, prices tumbled, and foreclosures increased dramatically.

Nonperforming commercial real estate loans increased from 2.9 percent in 1985, to 5.2 percent by 1991, as net charge-offs doubled to 1.6 percent over the same seven-year period. Commercial banks apparently relaxed lending standards in response to the increased competition from thrifts in this important lending space for commercial banks. The heightened competition that banks faced during the 1980s resulted from many factors, including: 1) the removal of deposit interest rate ceilings; 2) the granting of new lending authority to savings and loans; 3) the increase in the number of de novo savings and loan; 4) the shift from mutual savings institutions to stock ownership; and 5) a loss of a significant

Commercial Construction (Early 1990s)

Year	Commercial Construction Spending (Current Dollars)	Commercial Construction as Share of GDP (Percent of Nominal GDP)	Office Vacancy Rate (Percent)	Multifamily Housing Permits (Thousands)
1979	33.5	1.3	5.2	444.8
1980	41.0	1.5	3.4	365.7
1981	48.3	1.5	3.8	319.4
1982	55.8	1.7	5.5	365.8
1983	55.8	1.6	10.8	570.1
1984	70.6	1.8	13.1	616.8
1985	84.1	2.0	15.4	656.6
1986	80.9	1.8	16.5	583.5
1987	80.8	1.7	16.3	421.1
1988	86.3	1.7	16.3	386.1
1989	88.3	1.6	16.1	339.8
1990	87.5	1.5	16.7	262.6
1991	68.9	1.1	17.4	152.1
1992	64.5	1.0	18.8	138.4

Source: Is Commercial Real Estate Reliving the 1980s and early 1990s, Kansas City Fed Economic Review, Q3 2008

portion on commercial and industrial lending to the commercial paper market. As such, commercial real estate had become attractive to both commercial banks as well as thrifts, in part, because such loans came with large upfront fees that generated immediate income. These fees became an essential source of income to struggling institutions that competed aggressively to originate new loans.

The competitive link between thrifts and banks explains why the 1990–1991 recession was so deep, and why the recovery was so shallow. The aggressive competition for new lending, and the fees generated, led to a boom in commercial real estate that was followed by a bust as a second oil embargo brought with it renewed inflation fears and another spike in short-term rates. The result was the increased rate of failures, a collapse in credit availability, and a recession that only slowly released its grip on the economy. This broad-based banking/thrift problem was the first credit cycle of the postwar period.

Chapter 15

Corporate Governance Credit Cycle

The economic expansion that began in March 1991, and ended exactly a decade later, lasted one full year longer than the previous long postwar business cycle—the 1961–1969 expansion. The recession that punctuated this robust expansion was relatively short and shallow. In fact, it was similar to the mild 1969–1970 and 1990–1991 recessions that, respectively, followed the second and third longest expansions of the postwar period. Economists generally see the March–November 2001 recession as having been caused by an economy that had been weakened by a boom and then a bust in the technology sector, and to an explosion in capital spending on new technology. This left the economy with an overhang in such resources that became evident in the wake of the terrorist attacks of September 11, 2001.

This explanation, no matter how appealing on the surface, ignores the role that a breakdown in corporate governance had on the economy. The forced balance sheet adjustment following the accounting scandals at Enron, HealthSouth, Tyco International, and WorldCom rattled investor confidence as these once high-flying companies that had been held up as examples of excellence were downgraded to **junk status**, or had to file for Chapter 11 protection from creditors. Moreover, the distress in the merchant power industry was another important credit-related event that brought the longest expansion, to date, to its knees. Pacific Gas and Electric Company and Calpine, along with nine other key energy companies, got caught up in the race to produce technology company–like earnings by turning a once stodgy industry into a growth story, even if only temporarily. The corporate governance/accounting scandal/failed-growth company stories were all part of a credit-related bubble that burst, contracting liquidity to the economy, and triggering the recession.

The following analysis will highlight the challenges posed for the economy by these corporate events, and the effect they had on the financial markets. It was investors who created the credit crunch that led to the 2001 recession. The regulatory response to these transgressions will also be discussed, as well as the steps taken by other companies to avoid falling victim to the market dislocations that contributed to the recession.

The companies most identified with the 2001–2003 corporate governance scandals were Enron and WorldCom. These two high-flyers of the late 1990s were also most closely tied to the disruption in the commercial paper market that took the economy down. Enron, in fact, was forced to tap all of its bank backup credit lines to buy back $3.3 billion in short-term debt that it had difficulty rolling over. The company was also involved in the California energy crisis of 2000–2001, through its manipulation of the merchant power market. The resulting spike in wholesale electricity prices was critical in the failure of a number of electrical utilities, most notably Pacific Gas and Electric, and Calpine. Their failures amplified the disruption in the commercial paper market, and forced a balance sheet restructuring of the entire nonfinancial corporate sector. This forced balance sheet adjustment distracted companies long enough that the entire economy slipped into recession.

Enron was founded in 1985 from a merger between two relatively small regional energy companies, Houston Natural Gas Corp. and InterNorth Inc. Through a series of acquisitions, Enron grew into a major player in multiple markets for electricity, natural gas, communications, and pulp and paper. Six years later, on December 2, 2001, Enron filed for bankruptcy protection. Enron employed twenty thousand workers at its peak, and claimed to generate almost $111 billion in revenue in its 2000 fiscal year. The company principally was involved in transmitting and distributing electricity and natural gas throughout the United States. Enron developed, built, and operated power plants and pipelines that stretched from the Atlantic to the Pacific Ocean, and from border to border. This expansion was possible because of gains in Enron stock, and to protect this growth strategy, management eventually employed a number of questionable accounting tricks to hide its accumulating liabilities in a number of limited-liability, special-purpose entities. These accounting gimmicks kept the parent's balance sheet looking healthy, allowing it to report solid earnings and maintain a high credit rating. This shell game eventually became obvious, and the scheme surfaced in the media as analysts began to question the company's reported successes. Enron, which had been named "America's Most Innovative Company" six years in a row by *Fortune* magazine, unraveled rapidly, with its stock decreasing from $90.56 in the summer of 2000 to just pennies in 2001. This high-profile accounting scandal was just one of many that increased investor risk aversion, and pushed spreads significantly higher.

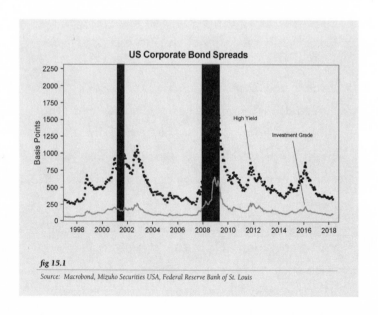

fig 15.1

Source: Macrobond, Mizuho Securities USA, Federal Reserve Bank of St. Louis

WorldCom, like Enron, was built through aggressive acquisitions, to become the country's largest Internet data provider, and its second largest long-distance company. Its CEO, Bernard Ebbers, had transformed a once obscure long-distance company into one of the nation's fastest-growing companies, through a series of sixty-five mergers in just a few years, the largest of which was the purchase of MCI Communications, for $37 billion. WorldCom, at its height, employed as many as sixty thousand workers across its various business lines. It grew to become one of the world's most valuable companies, worth more than $100 billion, and became the second largest long-distance company, behind only AT&T. Its fortunes began to decline in 1999 when businesses began to slash spending on telecommunications equipment. But the real problems for the company were the questions that arose when an internal audit discovered that the company's chief financial officer had improperly accounted for $3.8 billion in operating expenses, forcing the company to restate earnings. Additional investigations turned up $366 million in personal loans that the company made to its CEO that further complicated the viability of the company. The company had grown on the strength of its stock price, and when the scandal surfaced, the stock price plunged, and the company's debt became overwhelming. According to its Chapter 11 filing, WorldCom had $41 billion in debt on its books, $24 billion of which was in outstanding, marketable bonds. Although WorldCom's bankruptcy filing occurred in late 2001, banks that participated in the company's lending syndicate had expressed concerns about the company's finances early that year, and forced management to sell $12 billion in debt, to help protect its interest. This concern was also clearly evident in the widening experienced in corporate bond spreads.

The roots of the California electric crisis stretched back to the Public Utilities Regulatory Policies Act of 1978 (PURPA). This legislation was part of a broader National Energy Act that was intended to promote energy conservation and greater use of domestic energy, as well as renewable energy, to increase supply. These new regulations were intended to address the shortfalls in the industry that surfaced in the wake of the 1973 energy crisis.

PURPA had set the stage for the establishment of independent power producers to construct power plants, and contract directly with utilities and industrial users for electricity. Deregulated markets allowed these merchant power companies to trade electricity in a market in which prices could fluctuate, rather than remaining under traditional long-term fixed-rate contracts, used by regulated utilities. Through the late 1990s and early 2000s, the power industry experienced rapid growth, and Wall Street enthusiasm for financing this expansion added more fuel to the rapid expansion of merchant power providers. However, the partial deregulation of the electrical utility industry in California set the stage for a crisis. California kept caps on retail electric pricing, while allowing the wholesale price to be determined by the market. This resulted in shortages, multiple large-scale power outages, and an 800 percent spike in wholesale utility rates, between April and December 2000.

Prices spiked and shortages occurred, even though California had more installed capacity than peak demand. Illegal market manipulation by companies like Enron artificially created shortages by shutting down gas pipelines at times of peak electricity demand. Energy traders also took power plants offline, supposedly for maintenance, during periods of peak demand. The result was a margin squeeze on regulated utilities that caused the bankruptcy of Pacific Gas and Electric, the near bankruptcy of Southern California Edison, and a default on nearly $42 billion in debt by six energy providers in the region. This financial market distress was evident in the financial markets, most notably in a spike in the commercial paper spread. A sharp widening of spreads triggered a forced balance sheet restructuring across the entire nonfinancial space.

The principal forms of illegal manipulation consisted of megawatt laundering and overscheduling. The first of these illegal tricks is analogous to money laundering, in that providers obscure the true origins of electric power being sold in a market. The California energy market allowed for energy companies to charge utilities and industrial users more for energy generated out of state. It was therefore advantageous to make

Defaults Associated With California Energy Experience

	Defaults	Date of Default	Total Liabilities
1	York Research Corp	2001	223
2	Covanta Energy Corp (formerly Ogden)	2002	3,180
3	NRG	2002	10,657
4	PG&E NEGT	2003	8,927
5	Northwestern Corp (Montana Power)	2002/2003	3,129
6	Mirant	2003	16,460
	Total		42,576

Source: An Examination of Distress in the Electric Power Industry, Chris Ireland, NYU Stern School, 04/01/2015

it appear that electricity was being generated somewhere other than California. Because power lines have a maximum load that can be delivered at any time, transition lines need to be booked in advance, for transporting power between providers and users. Overscheduling is deliberately reserving more line usage than is actually needed, to force congestion fees to be added to the price. This practice was the basis for many of the strategies employed in manipulating the California market.

The disruptive effects of the California energy crisis were evident, well before Pacific Gas and Electric, and Enron filed for bankruptcy protection on April 7, 2001, and December 2, 2001, respectively. Problems began to surface in early 2001 when Pacific Gas and Electric failed to redeem commercial paper it had issued late in 2000. These promissory notes had been seen as safe investments and were purchased by many types of investors, including municipalities, counties, school districts, and pension funds, all of whom now had to address, not only the disruption in cash flow, but also the risk of default. The result was a sharp increase in the short-term cost of financing for all issuers, not just those involved in the California energy market. The A2/P2 commercial paper-spread increase, from as little as twenty basis points, in April 2000, to a peak of 125 basis points that December. This was the highest spread charged by investors since, the Federal Reserve began recording this spread.

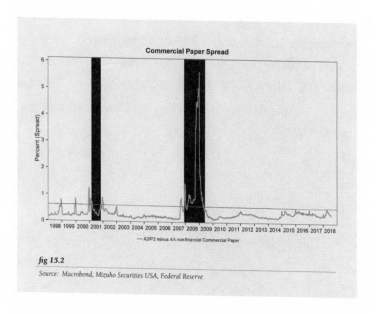

fig 15.2

Source: *Macrobond, Mizuho Securities USA, Federal Reserve*

The widening in this spread, and the unexpected accounting troubles, at a number of high-profile companies created a rush by other companies to clean up their balance sheets, to avoid being pulled down, as well. This forced management into a defensive posture, and the result was a credit-induced recession. Nonfinancial companies reacted by deleveraging and extending the duration of their liabilities. This restructuring not only lowered their debt burden, but it also reduced rollover risk—in other words, improving their balance sheets and further reducing their cost structures. Government regulators responded with the Sarbanes-Oxley Act, which imposed new corporate governance laws on all publicly traded US companies. The Securities and Exchange Commission approved additional corporate governance rules proposed by the New York Stock Exchange that increased CEOs' liability for the behavior of the companies they run, and separated security dealers' analysts from the investment banking side of their businesses. Additionally, the big accounting firms divested their consulting firms to avoid conflicts of interest in auditing.

Chapter 16

Subprime Credit Cycle

The linkages between financial dislocations and the business cycle were on full display in the eighteen-month-long recession that stretched between December 2007 and June 2009. As a result, this contraction proved to be, not only the longest, but also the deepest, of the postwar period, to date. The next longest recession lasted sixteen months, covering the period from July 1981 to November 1982. The decline in real GDP, from peak to trough, was initially placed at 4.2 percent, which was 0.6 percent deeper than that experienced during the eight-month August 1957 to April 1958 recession. Nonfarm payroll employment tumbled by 6.3 percent, eclipsing every prior recession. Only the 5.2 percent decline experienced in the November 1948 to October 1949 consolidation comes close. But the 17.1 percent contraction in industrial production far exceeded the 13.6 percent, and 13.1 percent declines recorded in the 1957–1958 and 1973–1975 recessions, respectively.

What made this recession so deep and so long is that two of the three important balance sheets underlying the economy were involved in its triggering. As always, the Federal

Reserve had been hiking rates prior to the downturn, but the key development that caused all the dominoes to fall was a decision by a government-sponsored enterprise (GSE), Freddie Mac, regarding its willingness to purchase high-risk mortgage-backed securities. This triggered a series of events that would burst a bubble that had been growing in the housing market for years. The housing bubble burst led to the failure, or forced the merger of several financial services companies, which severely curtailed liquidity in most domestic and international financial markets. As such, the 2007–2009 recession was linked to the global financial crisis, and included key aspects of every major financial debacle that preceded it.

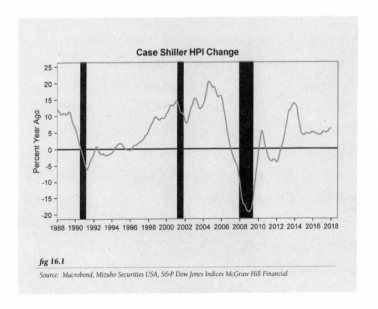

fig 16.1

Source: Macrobond, Mizuho Securities USA, S&P Dow Jones Indices McGraw Hill Financial

The chronology of both the micro and macro events that led to, and comprised, the crisis illustrates the scope of the problem—and how contagion turned a problem in the domestic mortgage market into a global financial crisis. The problems in the housing market first became evident in late 2005, as home prices, which had been climbing since 1998, began to decrease. Home prices had more than doubled from 1998 to 2005, far exceeding income growth, and reducing affordability. Securitization and the fee-generating aspects of mortgage originations facilitated the speculative aspect of the run-up in home prices. By bundling new issue mortgages and dicing up the cash flows into targeted securities, banks and other mortgage lenders could boost current earnings by increasing origination, and reducing balance sheet risk. As prices continued to rise, and origination increased, underwriting standards were eased, and troubles began to build as defaults rose. As such, the value of subprime mortgages rose, relative to the total pool of mortgages, to more than 20 percent by 2005–2006, from less than 7 percent in 2001. Subprime lending rose from about $185 billion to $625 billion over this same period. A study conducted by the Federal Reserve, post-crisis, shows that the spread premium charged by lenders to subprime borrowers fell dramatically, as the bubble inflated, declining from 2.8 percent in 2001, to just 1.3 percent in 2007, complementing the other factors that supported the bubble in residential building and mortgage origination.

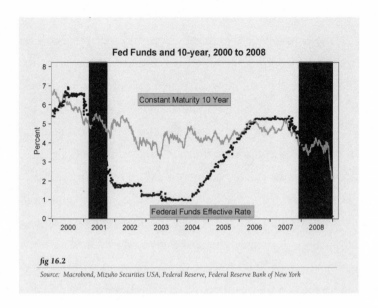

fig 16.2

Source: Macrobond, Mizuho Securities USA, Federal Reserve, Federal Reserve Bank of New York

Sustained low-interest rates between 1999 and 2004 made adjustable-rate mortgages more affordable, and attracted buyers who could not afford a traditional fixed-rate mortgage. The low initial (teaser) rate that banks could offer would-be buyers added to the speculative aspects of the housing bubble. Low rates were partially the result of the Fed's decision to hold short rates below 2 percent, between late 2001 and June 2004, in an effort to reverse the deflation pressures that surfaced following the 2001 recession. By the end of June 2004, these pressures had subsided, and the Fed embarked on a series of rate hikes that took the federal funds rate from 1 percent to 5.25 percent, by June 2006. A global savings glut prompted by the Asian financial crisis in 1997, amplified the effect of low rates, by increasing the demand for long-term Treasury debt. Policymakers in emerging markets reacted to

the Asian crisis by accumulating large current-account surpluses and reinvesting these funds into Treasury debt. The
resulting drop in long-term rates pushed investors into riskier,
higher-yielding assets to increase return, and for a healthy fee,
derivative mortgage-backed securities could be originated to
fit the risk-return profile that investors demanded. Inadequate
modeling of the risk implied in these securities increased their
attractiveness until defaults began to rise, and it became clear
that the ratings on these securitized products were inflated.

Following Freddie Mac's decision to no longer buy
high-risk mortgage securitizations, New Century Financial
Corporation, a leading mortgage lender to riskier borrowers,
filed for bankruptcy protection in April 2007. New Century
had been the second largest subprime lender at the beginning
of the year, but its "death spiral" was the result of its ware-
house lenders pulling credit lines. This caused New Century
to stop accepting mortgage applications.

The dislocations spread further in early May 2007 when
UBS had to close its Dillon Read Capital Management hedge
fund, after incurring a $125 million loss in its subprime
mortgage portfolio. Quickly thereafter, Moody's announced
it was reviewing its ratings on sixty-two tranches, based on
twenty-one mortgage securitizations. This process of rating
agency downgrades and losses accumulating on Wall Street
continued, and in the process, Bear Stearns had to provide
support to two failing hedge funds in June and July. Not long
after, Countrywide Financial, a large mortgage bank, was
forced to merge with Bank of America, after experiencing large

losses tied to subprime mortgages. In August 2007, two European banks were also forced to close hedge funds that were exposed to the US subprime problem.

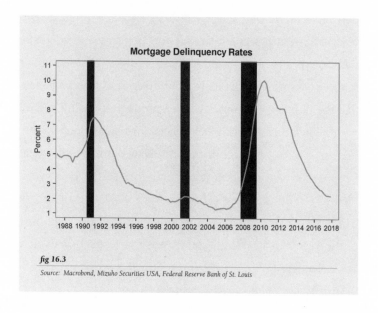

Mortgage Delinquency Rates

fig 16.3

Source: *Macrobond, Mizuho Securities USA, Federal Reserve Bank of St. Louis*

The subprime problem morphed into a full-fledged financial crisis in March 2008 when Bear Stearns was unable to recapitalize, due to losses in its mortgage-backed businesses, and its stock price collapsed. To avoid contagion risk, the Federal Reserve quickly orchestrated a government-sponsored bailout that saw the transfer of $30 billion in assets from Bear Stearns to a new investment company, created by the New York Fed. JPMorgan Chase bought what remained of Bear Stearns, at a deep discount. Bear Stearns' stock had traded at $93 a share just a month before it was merged, resulting in a huge loss for shareholders. The problem did not end there. As delinquencies continued to rise, mortgage lenders also faced problems, as the value of their collateral fell.

The most publicized casualty of these valuation problems was IndyMac, which specialized in originating Alt-A and other nontraditional mortgage loans (option adjustable-rate mortgages) on a large scale, in California and Florida. These limited documentation, low-quality, and complex loans were also financed with risky high costs, brokered deposits, and borrowings from the Federal Home Loan Bank Board. IndyMac's profitability was dependent on the securitization market, and as liquidity dried up, the drain from problem loans it had originated, pulled the mortgage bank down. In fact, when home prices fell in the second half of 2007, IndyMac was forced to hold some $10.7 billion in mortgage loans that it could not securitize, and get off its books. A rating downgrade by S&P in early July 2009 to **CCC** sealed the mortgage lender's fate, and the FDIC was forced to take over the bank, in conservatorship. With $32 billion in assets, IndyMac became one of the largest failures, second only to Continental Illinois.

The next dominoes to fall were Fannie Mae and Freddie Mac, which, together, owned about half of the outstanding mortgage market at that time—about $5.1 trillion in home loans. The two GSEs had raised $13.9 billion in spring 2008, but by September, continued losses forced both entities into Treasury conservatorship. The Treasury opted to stop paying the dividend on the GSEs' preferred stock when it assumed control of their operations, and this closed off another market that banks and securities firms typically used to raise capital—a step that exacerbated an already tenuous situation.

The collapse of the housing bubble and the subsequent downturn in the mortgage banking industry became a broader banking and financial services debacle in September and October 2008. The first casualty was the September 15 bankruptcy of Lehman Brothers and the $50 billion sale of Merrill Lynch to Bank of America. Illiquidity in the interbank lending market toppled Lehman and forced the Merrill merger. The following day, the Federal Reserve Board authorized the New York Fed to lend up to $85 billion to American International Group Inc. (AIG), a major insurer of credit default swaps (many default swaps were linked to derivative mortgage securities) that suffered an acute liquidity crisis. In an effort to stop the contagion, Goldman Sachs and Morgan Stanley became commercial banks on September 21 to gain access to the Federal Reserve's discount window, to reduce the risk of a liquidity squeeze that would bring these two investment banks down. A few days later, on September 25, the FDIC seized the assets of Washington Mutual, and transferred most of its assets to JPMorgan Chase. The final piece of the crisis fell into place before the end of September when Wells Fargo beat out Citigroup for troubled Wachovia. Underlying this collapse in the financial services and banking industries was the deterioration in household wealth that had inflated the housing bubble, and allowed households to buy more housing than they needed. When the eventual rise in defaults occurred, liquidity dried up, and the credit cycle became a self-reinforcing downturn.

The chronology of the subprime-related developments in the United States was mirrored overseas, making it truly an international financial crisis. Whereas the domestic leg was kicked off by Freddie Mac's decision to scale back its buying of subprime debt, the international side started with an unusual four-notch downgrade of securitized products, based on subprime mortgage debt, in June 2007. As a result, a more general review of the risk implied by subprime debt added to a growing uncertainty in the financial markets. The leverage that had been used (20:1) by the conduits and structured investment vehicles (SIVs) employed by most foreign investors to purchase these higher yielding mortgage derivative assets compounded the crisis by inflating the demand that motivated new origination. To fund these purchases, the conduits and SIVs issued commercial paper, which then added another aspect to the crisis—a collapse in the money markets. Rollover risk surfaced in the asset-backed commercial paper market in July 2007, and the crisis spread quickly.

The international aspects were evident, early on. Specifically, IKB Deutsche Industriebank AG's conduit had to draw down on its lines of credit from its parent, shortly after Bear Stearns announced that it was closing hedge funds it controlled that had bought structured mortgage-backed products. IKB had to be bailed out by its parent on August 7, 2007. Just two days later,

Top Domestic and International Corporate Write-downs Due to Subprime

Bank	Write-downs (Billion U.S.$)
Citigroup	46.40
Merrill Lynch	36.80
UBS	36.70
AIG	20.23
HSBC	18.70
RBS	16.50
IKB Deutsche	14.73
Bank of America	14.60
Morgan Stanley	11.70
Deutsche Bank	11.40
Ambac	9.22
Barclays	9.20
Wachovia	8.90
MBIA	8.41
Credit Suisse	8.13
Washington Mutual	8.10
HBOS	7.50

Source: Reuters, Federal Reserve Bank of St. Louis Review 9/10, 2005

BNP Paribas suspended withdrawals from three hedge funds that were heavily invested in collateralized debt obligations, based on subprime mortgage debt. BNP claimed it was unable to value its holdings because of how illiquid the market had become. A few days later,

on August 17, German bank Sachsen LB, failed to provide enough liquidity to support its conduit, Ormond
Quay, resulting in Landesbank Baden-Württemberg
taking over Sachsen LB. The global side of the crisis
really became front-page news that August after British
bank Northern Rock encountered funding difficulties,
and a run on its deposits caused the bank to fail. This
was the first UK bank, in 150 years, to fail as a result
of a run on its deposits. It wasn't until February 2008
that the Bank of England took over Northern Rock,
after repeated attempts to find a private sector solution.
Northern Rock's problem was a liquidity issue tied to a
collapse in the asset-backed commercial paper market.

To cushion the effect of the crisis on the economy and
to address specific market dislocations, the Federal Reserve
undertook a series of traditional and nontraditional policy steps. In fact, the makers of monetary policy repeatedly
invoked their emergency powers to authorize new, broad-
based programs to provide financial assistance to individual
institutions, in order to stabilize markets. Loans made by the
Federal Reserve peaked at more than $1 trillion in late 2008.

Traditional policy steps included the reduction in short-
term rates, and the Federal Reserve standing in as the lender's
last resort through its discount window. The federal funds rate
target was cut, through a series of ten consecutive steps, from
5.25 percent in September 2007, to a low of just twenty-five

basis points, by late December 2008. The Federal Open Market Committee also employed its ability to signal to the markets its intentions on the future direction of policy. To reduce uncertainty over the direction of rates, the Federal Reserve asserted that economic and inflation developments were "likely to warrant exceptionally low levels of the federal funds rate for an extended period." This unexpected step flattened the yield curve by pulling down forward rates.

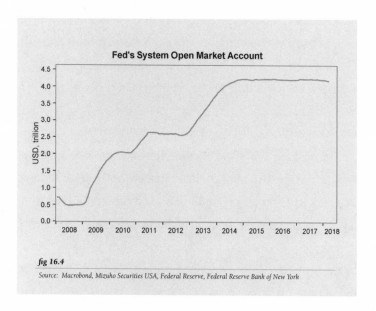

fig 16.4

Source: *Macrobond, Mizuho Securities USA, Federal Reserve, Federal Reserve Bank of New York*

The Federal Reserve's nontraditional policy initiatives took a big step forward, in December 2008, when it announced that it would begin to expand its balance sheet by purchasing up to $600 billion in agency mortgage-backed securities and agency debt in the market. On March 18, 2009, the Federal Open

Market Committee announced that this quantitative program would be expanded by an additional $750 billion, by purchasing agency mortgage-backed securities and agency debt, as well as $300 billion in traditional securities. This policy initiative has been called QE2 (see sidebar, "Nontraditional Monetary and Fiscal Policies Implemented," in Chapter 11). It began in November 2010 and lasted until June 2011, with an additional $600 billion in longer-dated Treasury securities. Operation Twist began on September 21, 2011, when the Federal Reserve announced a plan to purchase $400 billion in Treasury debt, with maturities between six and thirty years, and to sell a like amount of shorter-term Treasury debt, to lengthen the duration of its portfolio. This step was designed to flatten the yield curve, as short rates were pegged near zero. The final nontraditional easing was called QE3, and it was announced on September 13, 2012. QE3 was an open program of $40 billion a month in purchases of agency mortgage-backed securities. This purchase program was later expanded to include $45 billion a month in longer-term Treasury debt.

The dislocations that surfaced in a number of markets prompted the Federal Reserve to initiate a number of target programs to address the risk of illiquidity in those markets:

- TAF (Term Auction Facility) provided short-term loans to banks.

- DSL (Dollar Swap Lines) were designed to provide foreign central banks with US dollars.

- TSLF (Term Securities Lending Facility) provided loans of Treasury securities to primary dealers.

- PDCF (Primary Dealer Credit Facility) provided secured overnight loans to primary dealers.

- ABCP MMMF (Asset-Backed Commercial Paper Money Market Mutual Fund Liquidity Facility) provided loans to banks and their affiliates to purchase eligible, asset-backed commercial paper from money market mutual funds.

- CPFF (Commercial Paper Funding Facility) provided loans to special purpose vehicles to purchase new issue asset-backed commercial paper, as well as unsecured commercial paper from eligible issuers.

- TALF (Term Asset-Backed Securities Loan Facility) provided loans for the purchase of asset-backed securities, backed by autos, credit cards, education, and small business loans.

Direct assistance was also provided to Bear Stearns in order to facilitate its rescue by JPMorgan Chase, and to AIG, which needed government assistance to avoid bankruptcy. The Federal Reserve provided nonrecourse loans to Citigroup to ring-fence a pool of assets if losses on the portfolio exceeded $52.6 billion. Bank of America also received a nonrecourse loan to ring-fence losses on assets, if they exceeded $18 billion.

The scope of these traditional and nontraditional monetary policies reflected the fact that the subprime problem had morphed into a credit crunch, rivaled only by the Great Depression. If policymakers had not been so creative, the economic distress could have been substantially greater. This risk was highlighted by the length of time into the recovery that the Federal Reserve had to maintain near-zero short rates, and how much it had to expand its balance sheet to ensure that the economy had established a foundation solid enough that it could begin the long process of normalization.

Fannie Mae and Freddie Mac were placed into conservatorship by the Federal Housing Finance Agency on September 7, 2008, with the help of the US Treasury and the Federal Reserve. The fact that the financial crisis had its roots in the residential housing finance market has led to a view that the growth of these two entities was the catalyst behind the crisis. In hindsight, it is easy to see that the subprime crisis stemmed from rapid growth in nontraditional channels of housing finance. Specifically, the volume of mortgages financed by Fannie and Freddie between 2003 and 2007 was just 7.6 percent, while mortgage origination increased by 11.9 percent over this same period. On a cumulative basis, the overall mortgage market grew 31 percent faster than the volume of mortgages funded by the GSEs. This shift was the result of two developments: 1) the growth in private label mortgage origination was staggering at 219 percent, and 2) growth in the market was concentrated in subprime and Alt-A loans, which limited involvement in these types of loans, as they did not meet the GSEs' underwriting standards. The result was that the share of mortgages funded by the GSEs fell to 44 percent of the market in 2006, from 55 percent in 2002.

By the end of 2006, the volume of private label securitized mortgages had grown to more than $2.6 trillion (27 percent of all residential mortgage debt). The most dynamic period for the private label market was 2004 and 2005, when the private sector accounted for 49 percent and 45 percent of all originations, respectively. The private label market also specialized in issuing adjustable-rate and other riskier structures, to grab market share of the origination market. Fannie and Freddie did buy some of this private label debt for their portfolio, but only the AAA tranche. Fannie and Freddie were required to meet annual affordable housing goals set by the Department of Housing and Urban Development. This required the GSEs to purchase subprime and Alt-A debt in the secondary market, to the extent that the underlying mortgages were made for less-than-median-income households or collateralized by properties in "underserviced areas." The key to the private label market was hedge fund purchases of subordinated tranches, and money market funds that bought the asset-backed commercial paper, originated to fund the conduits. Foreign investors were also big purchasers of the various tranches carved out of each new issue in the hunt for yield.

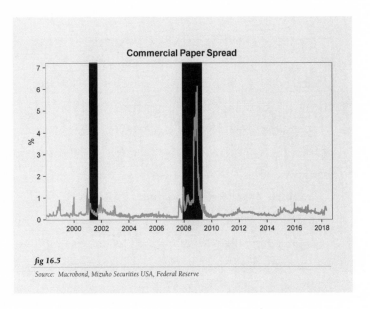

fig 16.5

Source: Macrobond, Mizuho Securities USA, Federal Reserve

As defaults on these nontraditional mortgages rose, even the AAA tranches purchased by the GSEs fell in value, and since their capital structure was thin, Fannie and Freddie quickly ran into capital problems. Because GSEs' debt had an implied government guarantee, due to their ability to borrow directly from the Treasury, capital adequacy concerns quickly became a political problem. Rising short-term rates and teaser rates used to attract a shrinking pool of qualified buyers were the keys to Fannie and Freddie's problems. Also, private label issuers had relaxed underwriting standards, especially those relating to documentation and deposits required to qualify for a mortgage. The rush to issue by these mortgage conduits led to no-document and zero-down mortgage originations. These conduits made their money through new origination and servicing fees, not by holding the mortgages in their portfolios. As the housing bubble burst, commercial paper spreads ballooned, and the value of collateral held by money market mutual funds fell, threatening the industry's liquidity and valuation promises.

Troubled Asset Relief Program (TARP) was a US government program designed to purchase toxic assets and equity from financial institutions to jump-start the restructuring process. The Emergency Economic Stabilization Act, which created the program, was signed into law by President George W. Bush on October 23, 2008, as the 2007–2009 financial crisis was still expanding its grip on the economy. TARP was designed to complement the raft of other programs initiated by the Federal Reserve and the Treasury, to address the subprime crisis, and was originally authorized to purchase up to $700 billion in distressed assets. The Dodd-Frank Wall Street Reform and Consumer Protection Act signed into law in 2010 cut the potential size of these purchases to $475 billion. The program allowed the Treasury to purchase from banks and other financial institutions, illiquid and difficult-to-value assets, such as collateralized debt obligation that were created during the bubble period to facilitate the origination of new mortgages. TARP was intended to improve liquidity of these assets by purchasing them in the secondary market to allow financial institutions to stabilize their balance sheets. The goal was to help banks stabilize their capital ratios and, by doing so, to stimulate new lending in the mortgage market that had shrunk considerably after the bubble burst, and banks faced increased foreclosures. In return for this help, financial companies were required to issue equity warrants, equity, or senior debt (in the case of nonpublic companies) to the Treasury so that the government could benefit in the turnaround of these institutions, and offset the cost of the bailout to taxpayers. General Motors and Chrysler, two nonfinancial companies that received aid, were loaned $18.4 billion as part of the bailout they received, in light of the auto industry's important role in the economy.

Chapter 17

International Financial Crises and Their Link to US Debacles

Not all financial crises have had their origin in the domestic economic cycle or deterioration in the domestic financial system. A handful of crises that originated in other countries and regions have also affected the US economy. It is this handful of crises that will be discussed in this chapter, as they serve to complement this analysis of the evolution of financial dislocations in the postwar period. Specifically, there are four important non-US crises that need to be discussed: 1) the Latin American debt crisis of 1982; 2) the Mexican peso crisis of 1984; 3) the 1987 Asian debt crisis; and 4) the Russian default in 1998. Other crises have occurred in the postwar period, besides these four, that while not discussed, are worth including in Table 17.1. These four international crises will be reviewed in chronological order so that each can be assessed against the economic backdrop that was covered in detail in the first eleven chapters.

Important Postwar Financial Crises

1982	Latin American Debt Crisis
1983	Israel Banking Crisis
1987	Black Monday
1989–91	Savings and Loan Crisis
1990	Collapse of Japanese Asset Price Bubble
1990–93	Finnish Banking Crisis
1994	Mexican Economic Crisis (Tequila Crisis)
1997	Asian Financial Crisis
1998	Russian Financial Crisis
2000–01	Dot-Com Bubble
2007–09	Subprime Financial Crisis

Source: Mizuho

The Latin American debt crisis of 1982 had its origins in the oil price shocks of the 1970s, and the recycling of petro-dollars that coincided with the rising wealth of the major oil exporting nations. The rapidly changing international financial markets of the 1970s created an unsustainable economic environment in Latin America, and planted the seeds for the crisis that would lead to a significant increase in default risks among South American governments and US commercial banks. Unprecedented access to cheap foreign capital in the form of low-cost, short-term borrowing encouraged Latin American governments and companies to overborrow. These imbalances were evident in financial flows and current account deficits, but did not boil over until Mexico announced that it would no longer be able to meet its debt-related obligations, in August 1982.

The anti-inflation policies advanced by the Federal Reserve, in reaction to the energy-induced wage-price spiral of the late 1970s, brought these debt imbalances to the surface. As a result, the re-pricing of default risk that followed on the back of Mexico's announcement resulted in a credit squeeze, forcing all other debtor nations in the region, such as Argentina, Brazil, and Chile, into financial distress. The resulting crisis required an international bailout involving the International Monetary Fund, the World Bank, the Organization of Economic Coop-eration and Development, and commercial banks with large exposure to the region.

US banks at the end of 1982 were significantly exposed to Latin American debt. The ones most identified with the crisis were Chase Manhattan, Manufacturers Hanover, and Citibank. Brookings Institute, at the time, estimated that the loans US banks originated in Latin America stood at 118 per-cent of bank capital, and for the nine largest banks, this ratio stood at 197.5 percent. This exposure would be amplified in the depth of the US recession triggered by the Volcker Fed's war on inflation.

In the period that followed the 1971 collapse of Bretton Woods—the postwar system of fixed exchange rates bench-marked to gold—the international community moved toward flexible exchange rates, and the result was unregulated growth in international capital markets and international banking. The economic shock brought about by OPEC's decision to hike energy prices, in the wake of the Yom Kippur War with Israel and the Iranian takeover by religious clerics, led to a significant shift in financial flows between oil-producing and oil-consuming countries. The sudden surge in flows overwhelmed OPEC's ability to spend or invest its new windfall, resulting in the balance of this surplus being deposited with international commercial banks. The recession in the US and Europe, caused by higher energy prices and rising short-term interest rates, made investing in developing nations very attractive for internationals banks which were flush with petrodollars needing to be put to work. Latin American countries needed these funds, as international lending agencies, such as the World Bank, were in the process of de-emphasizing their region in favor of areas with more pressing needs.

Commercial banks seized on this opportunity, and with strong capital flows into the region, local currencies appreciated and dramatically reduced the cost of funding new projects. The result was a significant shift from official long-term, fixed-rate borrowing, to short-term, floating rate borrowing, provided by international banks. The bulk of these funds were invested in long-term infrastructure projects, creating an asset-liability mismatch, and generating little in the way of cash flow to pay down the debt. By 1982, the regional foreign borrowing was mostly supplied by the private sector, with only 12 percent coming from official international institutions, down from over half, in 1961. Latin America, in fact, experienced a net capital inflow of between 17 percent and 20 percent annually

Changes in Bank Loan Exposure to Latin America, 1979–1986

Country	Percentage Change in Exposure, 1979–1982			Percentage Change in Exposure, 1982–1986		
	Total	Public	Private	Total	Public	Private
Argentina	71	165	41	4	84	-44
Bolivia	-31	-8	-54	-75	-70	-84
Brazil	50	78	38	10	92	-36
Chile	147	17	226	6	267	-50
Colombia	47	83	35	-33	19	-57
Costa Rica	-12	27	-35	-16	42	-81
Ecuador	29	22	33	7	147	-77
Guatemala	-47	57	-54	-60	27	-75
Honduras	-34	30	-57	-9	17	-38
Mexico	113	131	102	-3	50	-38
Nicaragua	-2	70	-76	-84	-84	-84
Panama	31	485	24	-61	-3	-65
Peru	82	27	139	-47	-2	-72
Uruguay	230	492	65	1	28	-59
Venezuela	34	28	38	-21	15	-47

Source: Federal Financial Institutions Examination Council, "Country Exposure Lending Survey," various issues, Brookings Papers on Economic Activity 2: 1987, Mizuho Securities

between the mid-1970s and 1982, when Mexico's announcement caused a credit squeeze that pushed the region over the edge. Per capita real GDP is estimated to have plunged by more than 9 percent between 1980 and 1985. To break this downward spiral, the International Money Fund quickly negotiated a bridge loan for Mexico, to avoid imminent default and buy time for a longer-term solution to be implemented. This eventually happened in 1989 with the adoption of the Brady debt relief plan that pooled these small, illiquid obligations, and replaced them with large, liquid dollar-denominated debt. The Latin American debt crisis reflects several of the same causes of the US financial debacles, particularly the reliance on short-term funding of long-term investments—an asset-liability mismatch that worked only as long as interest rates remained low.

. . .

The Mexican peso crisis ("Tequila Crisis") in 1994 is another important development in the evolution of financial crises in the United States, and one that would be repeated just a few years later in the 1997 Asian crisis. The lessons learned from these two currency-pegged debacles would inadvertently set the stage for the massive accumulation of official reserves, by emerging economies that ultimately played a key role in financing the US housing bubble that began to deflate in 2005. The Tequila Crisis also established a model for the international bailouts that would follow, and the constraints imposed on economies that mismanaged their macro policies. The constraint-imposed limits on these economies went well beyond the crisis period, and resulted in a global accumulation of excess savings that still influences the level of long-term interest rates, in the developed economies.

In the early 1990s, the Mexican economy seemed healthy and fully recovered from the lost decade ushered in by the Latin American debt crisis. Inflation was declining and the crawling peso peg seemed to be attracting foreign money into Mexico again, as trade barriers were being dismantled in accordance with the North American Free Trade Act (NAFTA) that had been signed by President Clinton. However, less than twelve months after NAFTA took effect, Mexico faced an economic disaster. The Mexican government was forced to abandon its dollar peg on December 22, 1994, and the financial crisis that followed cut the peso's value in half, sending inflation spiraling upward and triggering a deep and prolonged Mexican recession.

The evolution of the crisis is instrumental in understanding how global financial flows can magnify the effect of an economic imbalance—in this case, an overvalued currency—especially when combined with inappropriate financing decisions. For both the Mexican peso crisis and the Asian crisis, just three years later, a dependence on short-term funding from overseas investors brought a domestic collapse. Specifically, the Mexican government had adopted a crawling devaluation of the peso, relative to the dollar at a predetermined daily rate. What went wrong with this regime and the perception of stability that it implied was the fact that Mexico's inflation rate was consistently higher than the inflation rate in the United States, and the crawling peg did not adequately account for this divergence; the result was an overvalued peso. The currency overvaluation resulted in a growing trade deficit and a widening Mexican current account deficit. To finance this deficit and maintain the peg, the Mexican government borrowed heavily from foreign investors. This borrowing was accomplished through the sales of short-term, dollar-denominated government obligations called "tesobonos." These funds were then used to purchase pesos to maintain the crawling peg. The result was a rapid drawdown in Mexico's foreign currency reserves.

This drawdown of international reserves reached a critical juncture on December 20–21, when investors panicked and opted to redeem maturing tesobonos, instead of rolling them over. Mexico's foreign exchange reserves plunged by $4.6 billion, which was half of the government's stockpile. To stop the outflow, the Mexican government lifted the peg and allowed the peso to float on December 22. The result was rapid currency devaluation, spiraling inflation, and a spike in interest rates that resulted in a housing market collapse and a banking crisis. The peso depreciated roughly by 50 percent—from 3.4 pesos per

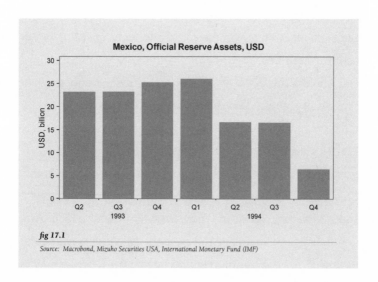

fig 17.1

Source: Macrobond, Mizuho Securities USA, International Monetary Fund (IMF)

dollar to 7.2—before recovering to 5.8, after the bailout. To avoid a Mexican default and provide the country with enough in foreign exchange reserves to improve confidence in its economy's ability to recover, the Clinton administration arranged a $50 billion bailout. The bailout overcame opposition in Congress, only because of growing fears of increased illegal immigration, and contagion to other Central and South American countries. The bailout was a collaboration between the US Treasury, International Money Fund, and the Bank for International Settlements.

Select Mexico Economic Statutes (1993–1996)

Year-on-Year Change (%)	1993	1994	1995	1996
Gross Domestic Product	2.5	4.8	-6.2	5.5
Volume of imports of G&S*	10.8	14.5	23.8	20.2
Volume of exports of G&S*	10.7	16.1	25.3	19.5
Unemployment rate (%)	3.4	3.7	6.2	5.5
Budget balance (% GDP)	0.2	-0.6	-4.2	-5.3
Current account balance (% GDP)	-4.8	-5.8	-0.5	-0.6
Inflation	9.8	7.0	35.1	34.3
GDP (PPP) per capita, USD	8,345	8,769	8,248	8,727
GDP per capita, USD current prices	5,578	5,732	3,675	4,181
*G&S: Goods & Services				

Source: IMF, Rabobank Economic Research

Economic imbalances, such as an overvalued currency, are typically apparent before they become a crisis, but when policymakers are unwilling to address the imbalances before they boil over, a crisis can result, as was the case in Mexico. The government repeatedly found excuses to justify the growing trade and current account deficits that clearly signaled the fact that the peso was overvalued. However, before investors rush to protect the value of their investments, a trigger is needed. In the peso crisis, it was a shift from the political calm of the Carlos Salinas de Gortari government, to the assassination of his handpicked successor, Luis Donaldo Colosio-Murrieta, and the violent revolt by the Zapatista Army of National Liberation, in the southern state of Chiapas. These developments caused a reassessment of risk in Mexico and a re-pricing of assets that highlighted the economic imbalances. Rising interest rates in the United States was another factor that accelerated the flow of money out of Mexico, as the sense of stability eroded. The evolution of this crisis also highlighted the fact that an economic contraction was not its cause. Instead, a run on the currency, due to an economic imbalance, led to a long, deep contraction in the economy.

. . .

Three years after the Mexican peso crisis, a similar financial and economic dislocation played out in Southeast Asia. In July 1997, the government of Thailand was forced to abandon its baht peg to the dollar. The currency peg had allowed Thailand and other ASEAN countries (Association of Southeast Asian

Nations) to attract significant foreign investments that quickly became unsustainable, relative to the size of the local economies. Foreign debt to GDP in ASEAN countries quickly rose to 167 percent, from 100 percent, between 1993 and 1996. To support the currency before the peg was broken, a dramatic increase in short-term interest rates was made to attract a steady flow of overseas investment. High and rising short-term interest rates, however, resulted in a collapse in the economy, making the foreign debt burden unserviceable, which deepened the recession. As with the Latin American and peso crises, a financial imbalance triggered the turn in the business cycle, rather than of the other way around.

The credit squeeze that gripped Thailand was repeated in additional Southeast Asian countries. A currency-induced credit crunch crisis spread across the region to Indonesia, South Korea, Hong Kong, Laos, Malaysia, and the Philippines. Countries less affected by the crisis were Brunei, China, Singapore, Taiwan, and Vietnam. The crisis was so far reaching that even Japan felt its effects. The toxic mix of currency pegs, unsustainably high foreign debt, rising US short-term rates, and the US jobless recovery of the early 1990s gave way to a more sustainable growth trajectory that caused investment funds to leave the region—opening up the currency pegs to speculative assaults from hedge funds. Investors lost confidence in the region's economic model. It was based on high domestic interest rates to attract strong foreign capital flows that then powered growth rates of 8 percent to 12 percent annually, which proved to be unsustainable. Investors' confidence was not restored until the International Money Fund initiated a $40 billion bailout for the worst-hit countries.

. . .

The International Money Fund and World Bank were forced to cobble together another rescue package in July 1998 to support necessary economic reforms in Russia, after the Kremlin was forced to abandon its ruble peg, despite interest rates having been bumped up to 150 percent, at the peak of the Russian debacle. The seeds of the Russian default (ruble crisis) were a fixed exchange rate implemented by the Russian government to sustain foreign capital flows, despite the political instability of the Yeltsin era, a chronic fiscal deficit, and an economy based on oil and other raw materials that was hit as commodity prices plunged, in the wake of the Asian crisis. As such, the 1998 Russian debacle represented contagion from the Asian financial meltdown.

Current Account Balances (Billions of U.S. Dollars)

Country or Region	2000	2006	2010	2013
Advanced Economies	-269.1	-485.1	-38.8	157.1
United States	-410.8	-806.7	-443.9	-400.3
Japan	130.7	174.5	217.6	33.6
Euro area (Sum of 18 EA countries)	-36.4	44.4	59.4	356.0

France	19.3	-13.0	-33.8	-36.9
Germany	-34.2	173.4	194.6	254.9
All Peripheral Europe (GIIPS)	-47.8	-197.8	-186.0	44.2
Italy	-2.2	-27.5	-70.3	20.5
Spain	-23.1	-110.9	-62.3	10.6
Other Advanced Economies (ex Asia)	47.4	102.7	128.0	167.7
Australia	-15.6	-45.3	-44.6	-49.9
Switzerland	31.4	57.6	78.7	103.9
United Kingdom	-42.9	-70.7	-61.9	-113.8
Canada	18.6	17.9	-56.7	-58.5
Emerging Markets	**134.9**	**730.1**	**467.2**	**429.7**
Asia	79.8	364.0	377.9	336.9
China	20.4	231.8	237.8	182.8
Thailand	9.3	2.3	10.0	-2.5
Hong Kong	7.5	24.6	16.0	5.1
Korea	10.4	3.6	28.9	79.9
Taiwan	8.9	26.3	39.9	57.3
Singapore	10.2	36.9	55.9	54.6
Latin America and the Caribbean	-48.5	46.2	-63.7	-152.5
Argentina	-9.0	7.2	-1.2	-4.9
Brazil	-24.2	13.6	-47.3	-81.1
Mexico	-18.8	-7.8	-3.9	-25.9
Mideast, North Africa, Afghanistan and Pakistan	80.6	280.6	178.6	341.2
Sub Saharan Africa	3.4	29.5	-10.2	-38.5

continued

Eastern Europe	-28.5	-84.1	-84.5	-74.5
Former Soviet Union	48.1	93.9	69.1	17.0
Excess Demand (-)/Excess Saving (+)	**-134.2**	**245.0**	**428.3**	**586.8**

Source: IMF, Brookings "Why are Interest Rates so Low," Ben Bernanke

A primary result of the Asian financial crisis and the Russian default was a sharp reduction in risk tolerance by countries in the region—a shift from excess borrowing in order to fund rapid growth, and increased investments, to a preference for savings and efficiency gains. This shift in the flow of funds was evident in the growth of sovereign wealth funds among emerging economies and in the current account data. Between 2000 and 2006, the emerging economies increased their current account surplus from $134.9 billion to $730.1 billion, an increase of more than $595 billion. In contrast, the advanced economies increased their net borrowing by only $216 billion. The difference is a good estimate of how much excess savings were being generated in the global economy. The owners of these increasing saving balances were also looking for high-return investments in which to grow their wealth further. It was this savings glut that helped finance, among other things, the US housing bubble. Excess savings, largely composed of US dollars and euros, were recycled into the Treasury and peripheral European debt, resulting in decidedly lower long-term interest rates. The search for yield was a key contributor to the investment community's decision to originate the derivative securities that were at the heart of the financial crisis of 2007–2009.

Conclusion

The principal thought to take away from this review of US recessions and financial debacles is that the driver of business cycles has evolved over the postwar period. Although business cycles still tend to be triggered by a monetary policy mistake, the transmission mechanism has shifted from the goods markets to the financial markets. More to the point, as the global economy transitioned from a world of excess demand to that of excess supply, recessions have come to be driven by financial dislocations, and not disruptions in the goods markets.

Immediately after World War II, an inflation-induced tightening by the Fed led to a disintermediation of the banking system, and an associated credit crunch that caused demand to contract. A recession followed. This contraction in the economy subsequently caused a one-off financial hiccup, as rising short-term rates caused problems to surface in the weakest institutions, and led to either bankruptcy or bailout, depending on the size and importance of the institution. As the postwar period matured, business cycle dynamics changed. Each of the past three business cycles, in fact, resulted from a financial accident rather than a sudden cutback in aggregate demand. The contraction in liquidity led to reduced demand, but the causality has shifted.

The nine business cycles spanning the period from November 1945 to June 1990 were essentially inflation cycles. Inflation picked up as expansion pushed the economy against its capacity constraints, and the Federal Reserve responded by hiking rates, slowly at first, but as inflation pressures continued to build, the pace of tightening accelerated. Eventually, rising short-term rates overtook rising long-term rates, resulting in a yield curve inversion, and banks began to contract credit. The demand for goods slowed as rising rates induced increased savings, and reduced borrowing, when banks became reluctant to lend.

In the recessions immediately following World War II, each recession was punctuated by a small number of bank failures, primarily due to fraud, as desperate times tend to lead people to desperate measures. As the postwar period extended, fraud turned into inappropriate lending as the primary driver of financial debacles, caused by recessions. The complexity of bank failures gradually increased and extended into problems in liability management. These banking dislocations evolved further into international incidents such as those associated with the failure of Franklin National, in 1974. Franklin expanded by borrowing in the brokered market, and used its overseas branch network to borrow from overseas investors by using innovative, new liabilities that it pioneered. As its funding costs increased in the wake of growing concern over its energy-related assets in a declining market for crude, management tried to cover its losses by speculating in the currency markets, and its eventual failure was felt in many countries.

The size of bank failures also expanded as the postwar period progressed. As a result, the first government-sponsored bailout of a national bank occurred in March 1980, on the back of the very next recession. The bailout of First Pennsylvania Bank N.A. was the only course of action available to regulators, at the time, that would not undermine confidence in the financial system. This is the first example of systemic risk in the postwar period. The mistake made by the bank's management was the classic "goof"—betting the wrong way on interest rates through its portfolio of government bonds and its involvement in real estate investment trusts. These assets were also funded with expensive and unreliable short-term deposit liabilities, adding an asset-liability mismatch on top of inappropriate lending as a reason for its failure.

The 1980 recession was followed very quickly by the deep, protracted 1981–1982 economic downturn that exposed the excessive concentration of energy-related lending at Penn Square Bank N.A. This Oklahoma-based financial institution failed on July 5, 1982, around the height of the recession, and proved to be the first bank failure since the FDIC was established, in which uninsured deposits had to absorb the losses. The Latin American debt crisis could also be included as another result of this recession, as rising short-term rates in the United States triggered devaluation in the peso, causing a run on Latin American banks. This was also the first time that changing economic conditions led to an industry-wide banking crisis. Most banks in the region felt the brunt of the associated illiquidity, resulting in a major international bail-out. These developments reflect the continuing evolution of financial dislocations that eventually reversed the causality between recessions and credit debacles.

The next major step toward the credit cycle (financial accident) leading the business cycle was the collapse of the thrift industry. The problem at thrifts (savings and loans) can be traced to problems beyond the Federal Reserve's anticipatory tightening, to forestall inflation as the expansion grew long in the tooth. Deregulation and the government's attempts to allow the industry time to grow out of its problems, rather than confronting the ramifications of a hit to the housing finance industry, created a competitive environment that deepened the industry's troubles, resulting in rising defaults. The demise of the industry coincided with the recession, and at the time, it was perceived to have been triggered by the recession. But, in retrospect, rising nonperforming loans and the associated cut-back in available credit to the important construction industry contributed to the depth of the recession and the shallow job-less recovery that followed.

The Dot-Com recession was the first postwar business cycle principally credited to a financial market dislocation. The general perception was that the mild 2000–2001 recession was caused by a bursting of the equity market bubble, predicated on the technology boom and the so-called virtuous cycle created by investment in new technology. Accelerated investment in, and adoption of, new technology were seen as constraints on inflation as productivity expanded, leading to earnings growth and further investments in this area. The explosion in tech valuation triggered a bubble in Dot-Com stocks that stretched valuations to the point that fundamentals no longer mattered, and speculation took over.

All speculative bubbles burst, and when the NASDAQ tumbled, the wealth destruction was unprecedented, and economists were quick to blame the recession on the associated loss in confidence. The real catalyst for the recession was the collapse of the independent power market and the accounting scandals that rocked a number of high-flying companies that had used deception to hide the debt they had accumulated in the rush to show that their growth rivaled that of technology companies. The speed at which markets allowed heavily indebted companies to term out their short-term debt into longer maturities in a declining rates environment—caused by the recession—substantially reduced the damage to the real economy. The September 11 attacks, and the government's strong fiscal position going into the downturn, also allowed a pro-cyclical fiscal stimulus to be undertaken by the George W. Bush administration. Because inflation never really surfaced during the April 1991–February 2001 expansion, rates were able to drop to unexpected levels during the recession, and remain unusually low in the following upturn. This low yield environment set the stage for the subprime crisis that would cause the next, and last, postwar recession to date. The global excess supply of savings created a global search for yield that fed the housing bubble and added to the international aspect of the crisis. The failure of a number of key financial institutions, both domestically and internationally, in rapid succession, added a systemic twist to the subprime debacle.

The US housing bubble began to deflate in 2005, as default rates rose on the riskier mortgage loans that had been originated late in the bubble period. Initially, the cost of rising defaults was offset by increased origination of new product. Essentially, losses could be covered if the fees generated from new loans were large enough. This created an incentive to cut corners in the lending process, and originate loans that should never have been underwritten. The use of off–balance sheet entities to expand leverage also delayed the onset of the crisis, but also amplified the magnitude of the growing problem. As losses accumulated, the rating agencies began to question the quality of the loans that were being made, and the structures used to distribute the new-issue products to investors. As a result of this shift in risk tolerance, the liquidity to the economy began to dry up, and as the economy began to slow, the housing bubble burst, and inflated home prices began to drop. Homeowners' equity was wiped out and defaults reached high levels. The destruction of wealth led to a deterioration in household balance sheets. The losses at financial institutions began to accelerate after several hedge funds were shut down by their parent financial institutions in a panicky attempt to stem the rising tide of withdrawals and losses from distressed sales of increasingly illiquid assets.

The real problems for the markets and the economy became evident when Bear Stearns succumbed to a liquidity squeeze, as investors refused to lend the investment bank enough to finance its portfolio of mortgage-related assets. The shotgun merger with JPMorgan Chase triggered a series of events that rippled through the domestic and global banking systems, deepening the recession domestically and internationally. The crisis in confidence triggered by the Bear Stearns situation was magnified through the asset-backed commercial paper market, and problems quickly surfaced at Lehman Brothers, AIG, Fannie Mae and Freddie Mac, and Citigroup. Overseas banks were not immune, as problems surfaced in the United Kingdom, Germany, France, the Netherlands, and even Iceland. As such, the bursting of the US housing bubble spread from institution to institution and from North America to Europe and Southeast Asia. The resulting global recession depressed commodity prices and pulled emerging economies down with their more advanced neighbors.

Deterioration in household balance sheets also dragged down the banking industry's balance sheets, making this the first financial disruption since the Great Depression that involved two key macro balance sheets—the household sector and the financial sector. This unprecedented postwar disruption threatened deflation, and required the development and implementation of new and innovative monetary and fiscal policy initiatives, to arrest the contagion and give the economy time to find its footing. The subprime crisis completed the evolution from one-off financial dislocations, or symptomatic failures, on the back of recessions, to a systemic financial market disruption, leading to a global recession.

The lessons learned from this historical analysis suggest that the risk of future recessions will become evident in the financial data long before they surface in the goods markets. Evaluating the underlying health of the key macro balance sheets will provide clues as to where problems may surface, and the likely timing of the next contraction. Evaluating the balance sheets of the banking and financial service industry, the household sector, and the nonfinancial corporate sector will tell more about the state of the expansion than assessing capacity constraints in a world of excess supply. History also shows that all debacles involve some combination of the following imbalances: an increase in leverage, an asset-liability mismatch, a reliance on some form of brokered financing, rising debt burden, and a shift away from fundamental valuation metrics. It is also interesting that all three of the postwar credit cycles—the 1990–2009 cycles—involved a breakdown in the commercial paper space. The analysis presented also shows that conditions domestically and internationally can have serious implications for the domestic and global economy. The biggest imbalance, as of this writing, may prove to be the global imbalance in trade and associated financial flows if governments pursue inappropriate policy decisions.

Acknowledgments

A number of colleagues and old friends deserve to be identified for their contribution to this study of the evolution of financial debacles in the US during the postwar period. Specifically, the contribution of Tetsuo "Harry" Ishihara needs to be recognized. Harry's organizational skills, dedication, and research abilities were truly invaluable in compiling the information necessary to complete this study. The editing skills of a dear friend, Seton Seremba Brown, also need to be highlighted. Seton has been my go-to person for years, and she has never let me down. My thanks go out to Kurt Switala for his fast compliance review and content suggestions. Special thanks to the management of Mizuho Securitas USA LLC for indulging my desire to dig into our country's economic history and explore the lessons history can teach us about the future. I would like to thank my family for their support, patience, and understanding. Finally, the coordination skills of Ashley Horne also need to be mentioned, as they proved to be invaluable to me.

About the Author

Steven Ricchiuto has worked on Wall Street since 1980, as an economist, strategist, and a director of fixed income research. He worked at several firms prior to joining Mizuho Securities USA LLC, including Donaldson, Lufkin and Jenrette; Kidder Peabody; and Dean Witter. He also worked in the US securities arms of several large European Banks, such as Barclays; ABN AMRO; and Svenska Handelsbanken. He is currently the US economist at Mizuho Securities USA LLC.